IN MY ANECDOTAGE

Tales from a very long life

by

Dennis Glauber

ISBN: 9798835267583

First Edition

DEDICATION

This volume is dedicated to three ladies whose inspiration, assistance and encouragement have been indispensable. In early 1998, soon after my retirement, I joined the Temple Beth Am (Seattle) Prime Time Writers group founded by my dear friend Marilyn Layton. Over the next fifteen years I benefited from her extraordinary wise and probing advice and stimulation. Now, thanks to Zoom, I am again able to interact with and learn from this admirable teacher and instructor. Thank you, Marilyn.

My good friend Miranda McPhee has been absolutely indispensable in bringing this project to fruition. I am in awe of her amazing cheerful efficiency in urging me to take the plunge into publication, and her brisk guidance through the many thickets that confront a ninety-five-year-old novice writer. Many many thanks.

To my dear wife, Evette, I can only express appreciation and humble gratitude for all the support, encouragement and love that we have shared in this and every project in our lives together. Thanks beyond words.

Laguna Woods, CA
July 2022

ACKNOWLEDGEMENTS

Many of the pieces in this volume were originally published in issues of Laguna Woods Village Stories between 2015 and 2021. I am grateful to Peggy Edwards and team members of the Publishing Club for making that possible.

I gratefully acknowledge the skill of my beloved daughter, Barbara Lindenberg, for designing the front and back covers.

CONTENTS

THE POWER OF THREE

My book group has recently been engaged in a fascinating work of fiction. It is an historical novel written in three parts featuring three protagonists living in the same area of Provence in three different eras—the declining Roman Empire of the fifth century waiting for the Barbarians, the mid-fourteenth century of the Black Death and the papal exile from Rome, and finally the turbulent first half of the twentieth century.

The legacies and impact of the three "heroes" and the interweaving of their lives and times demands and receives fine writing. I could not help noticing that some of that fine writing derives from the author's penchant for using phrases, clauses or words in clusters of three, or triads.

He does this again and again and again, but let me cite just a few examples:

"She had comforted him, reassured him, stilled his heart"
"His father had been foolish, too trusting, too merciful"
"When to give, how to give, what to give"
"And compete for favor, influence and fortune."

Now, was it my own preoccupation with the prevalence of threes in our consciousness that made lines like these leap off the page, or has the author tapped into a rhythm that is basic to our lives, a rhythm that is natural, pleasing and harmonious? So let me expand on what I call the Power of Three

We could begin with the Holy Trinity of Father, Son and Holy Spirit, and we need no reminding of the number of Magi who attended that particular birth. But long before the Christian tradition there were the three Hebrew patriarchs Abraham, Isaac and Jacob, while Classical Mythology gave us the Three Graces, the Three

Fates and the Three Furies, to which late twentieth century culture added the Three Tenors. Consider some of the phrases which have become an integral part of our language and culture:

"Life, liberty and the pursuit of happiness"
"Of the people, by the people, for the people"
"Hear no evil, see no evil, speak no evil"
"Three cheers for the red, white and blue"
(and each cheer is itself a triad of hip, hip, hurrah)
 "Three strikes and you're out"
"By bell, book and candle"
"Niña, Pinta and Santa Maria"
"Bed Bath and Beyond" (benefiting by being
beautifully alliterative).

And of course, the triples are not just in English—

"Liberté, Egalité, Fraternité"
"Veni, vidi, vici"
"E pluribus unum"
 "In vino veritas."

The impact of the power of three on all of us begins even before we are born. The nine-month period of gestation is divided into three trimesters. It continues as we learn our ABCs and move on to the three Rs. Our nursery rhymes introduced us to the three blind mice, Goldilocks and the three bears, the big bad wolf and the three little pigs. What parent didn't get us to tidy our rooms or perform some chore by threatening "I'm just going to count to three"? And when I say "we," I mean all of us—every Tom, Dick and Harry. You, you and you. Yes you, the long and the short and the tall; and yes you, the good the bad and the ugly; the butcher, the baker, the candlestick maker, not forgetting the waiter, the porter and the upstairs maid.

10

Didn't we all laugh with the Three Stooges, and thrill with the Three Musketeers? Didn't we all hope to find the magic lamp with the genie who would grant us three wishes? And is there a jockey, a trainer or an owner who doesn't dream of winning the Triple Crown—the Derby, the Belmont, the Preakness? Has there ever been a swimmer, a skater or a sprinter who has not aspired to the triad of Gold, Silver, Bronze at the Olympic Games, the Olympics whose motto is just three words:

CITIUS, ALTIUS, FORTIUS
(Latin for Faster, Higher, Stronger)

The power of three pervades our culture morning, noon and night. Shakespeare's *Macbeth* opens with the Three Witches intoning "when shall we three meet again," but also has the Three Murderers and the Three Apparitions to further the plot (and Lady Macbeth's plot). And of course, there is always "tomorrow and tomorrow and tomorrow."

Mozart's *Magic Flute* has the Three Ladies who punish Papageno for lying, the Three Boys who lead our heroes to Sarastro and to the Three Temples dedicated to WISDOM, REASON and NATURE as well as the ordeal of the Three Trials before the inevitable happy ending.

Classical music leans heavily on sonata form with its three parts of exposition, development and recapitulation. In the world of art, at Sotheby's auction in New York in 2013, a record trifling $142 million bought what else but a triptych! (By Francis Bacon—three studies of Lucien Freud.) And no doubt the auctioneer used the traditional "going for the first time, going for the second time, going for the third and last…"

The Russians call it a troika—rule by three or three horses in harness. Pre-Imperial Rome in its heyday was ruled not by one but by two triumvirates at different times. And similarly, post–revolutionary France was ruled by a three-man Consulate before one of them decided to make the country over in his own Napoleonic image.

So, the Power of Three is so ingrained as to be almost part of our DNA.

DNA, now there's THE three-letter abbreviation for our era. So, adieu, farewell and adios to those three-letter buzzwords of bygone eras—DDT, LSD and the unlamented KKK.

For sending me off in three directions I have to say that my admiration for author IAIN PEARS is genuine, enthusiastic and boundless.

As for the book itself, well all in all, if truth be told, as a matter of fact, *The Dream of Scipio* is educational, erudite and entertaining!

And I am

DENNIS TEDDY GLAUBER

NATIONAL BESTSELLER

IAIN PEARS

·AUTHOR OF·

AN INSTANCE OF THE FINGERPOST

The Dream of Scipio

"A thrilling journey through history, into
the human heart and soul." —*The Washington Post*

The book that inspired the essay
"The Power of Three."

A NARROW ESCAPE

This essay concerns my family's arrival in South Africa from Europe in the late nineteenth and early twentieth centuries, and so a very brief history of the South Africa into which I was born is perhaps appropriate. Portuguese explorers first "discovered" the southern tip of the continent in the late fifteenth century; in 1652 the Dutch East India Company established a settlement in what is now Cape Town as a way station en route to Batavia; the British first appeared on the scene during the Napoleonic Wars at the turn of the nineteenth century. Under British control slavery was abolished in 1832 and so a significant number of the Dutch-speaking (later Afrikaans-speaking) population moved north to the interior. Throughout this period there were frequent clashes and frontier wars with the indigenous black tribes, whose civil rights were largely ignored by both sides of the minority white population.

Two major events of the nineteenth century led to a wave of immigration from all parts of Europe. The discovery of extensive diamond fields in the 1860/70s was followed in 1886 by the finding of the most abundant deposits of gold anywhere in the world. Among the tens of thousands seeking a new life and potential riches in this remote but exciting part of the world were numerous Jews from Eastern Europe. While millions of Jews were leaving Czarist oppression for the beckoning shores of America, thousands, especially from Lithuania, Latvia and Poland headed south to find their fortune. My father, a teenager from a Lithuanian *shtetl*, was among them. The defining event prior the formation of the Union of South Africa in 1910 was the Anglo-Boer war of 1899-1902, fought largely to give the British access to and control of the immensely rich underground treasures in the Boer Republics.

My mother was born and raised in the coastal city of Memel in what is now Lithuania but was then part of East Prussia. She arrived in South Africa in 1914, met and married my father the following year, and raised a family of three boys of whom I, born in 1927, was the youngest.

In 1931, when I was just four years old, my father still in his early fifties succumbed to cancer. Our house, the home in which we three boys had all been born, was quickly sold and my mother decided to pay an extended visit to her elderly parents in Lithuania. I have vague memories of the voyage to England on the SS Carnarvon Castle, of being sick on the cross-channel trip from Dover to Ostend, and clearer memories of my uncle's house in Frankfurt where we stayed for some weeks. I was enrolled in kindergarten there and recall the puzzlement of some of the other kids at this little boy who came from Africa but wasn't black!

We must have spent many weeks in the family home in Memel. I recall the sandy beaches and the prevalence of horse-drawn carts and the resulting droppings littering the streets. One day my mother made a momentous decision. Still grieving for her beloved husband and feeling that for her, there was no reason to return to South Africa, she announced her intention to remain with her parents and sisters in the land of her birth. Therein lies the "narrow escape" of the title of this memoir. Thankfully, wiser heads prevailed. This was 1932 and just across the border the Nazi party had recently secured their largest vote ever, only a few months before Hitler assumed total power. I don't know exactly who it was who convinced my mother "You get yourself and your kids out of here NOW, and you take your youngest sister with you, d'you hear?"

Thank heavens, she heard and heeded. My unmarried aunt sailed with us back to safety in South Africa. My mother corresponded regularly with her remaining sister until June 1941and the German invasion. Thereafter, silence. My aunt, her husband and children were all among the 6,000,000 who perished. And as I write this at the end of January 2022 and we commemorate yet another Holocaust Memorial Day, I thank whatever gods may be that I and my family lived to tell the tale of a very narrow escape.

THERE'S BEEN AN ACCIDENT!

The telephone call came through at about seven thirty that evening. Of course, I can never forget the date, August 31, 1950, only two months and four days after my marriage to my beloved Ruth and just four days after her twenty-second birthday. The message was ominous and urgent. "Get yourself to the General Hospital immediately. Your wife has been in an accident. She has a fractured skull and possibly a fractured cervical spine."

This was back in our hometown of Johannesburg, South Africa. I was a recent medical graduate doing my internship year at the giant Baragwanath Hospital, the teaching hospital serving the black townships of Soweto, about ten miles southwest of Johannesburg. Being on surgical call that night, I had used hospital transport to get to work that day, leaving our little car for Ruth's use.

How to get back to the General Hospital in downtown Johannesburg at that hour? Fortunately, two women medical students had driven out to Baragwanath hospital for an evening of extra experience in emergency and trauma, of which there was an abundance. They were more than willing to drive me, fast, to the "Gen" as the General Hospital was called. A possible cervical spinal fracture, a broken neck, possible quadriplegia. To this day, more than sixty-five years later, I am chilled and horrified as I recall my determination that rather than see her doomed to life as a quadriplegic, I would somehow contrive to cut that life short, and my own as well.

Happily, those terrifying fears were unrealized. Her neck was not broken, and the injury was restricted to a fracture of the base of her skull in the petrous temporal bone, through which runs the auditory nerve responsible for hearing. Prior to the introduction of antibiotics just a few years earlier such fractures which, like hers, involved leakage of spinal fluid through the ear, frequently led to meningitis which was usually fatal. Alexander Fleming's penicillin saved Ruth Glauber's life. But the fracture had severed the auditory nerve. As predicted, the extreme vertigo gradually disappeared entirely but as also predicted, the deafness was total, untreatable and permanent.

The details of the accident emerged. With me being away for the night, Ruth had accepted an invitation to have dinner with a friend from work, Eileen, and her student husband. Eileen was seven months pregnant at the time. She picked Ruth up for the drive to the Married Students Residence. It was a moonless, rainy night and in those days there were no reflective strips on the back of heavy vehicles. Thus it was, that Eileen did not see the parked truck until the very last moment, veered unsuccessfully to avoid the collision, and so Ruth received the full brunt of the blow. Seatbelts were of course unknown in 1950. Eileen was completely unhurt and fortunately did not go into premature labor.

When urged that we had to sue Eileen and her husband, Sonny, we protested. They lived in student housing and were probably as impecunious as we were. Assured that it was not a personal matter but a case of one insurance company suing another, we proceeded. Now this is the part that will amaze you, possibly appall you and probably amuse you. For pain and suffering and the handicap of permanent unilateral deafness in a twenty-two-year-old with a probable sixty years of life (unfortunately not fulfilled) ahead of her, our lawyer was pleased that we were awarded, wait for it, the grand total of £1,100, the equivalent then of $4,400! Admittedly, this was 1950, but I have little doubt that even then the award, had we been in the US, would have been several orders of magnitude larger.

We lost touch completely with Eileen and Sonny, not through any animosity, but they moved to Cape Town a thousand miles away and our separate lives went on.

Fast forward now about fifty years. Our daughter Barbara, living in Houston, TX, mentioned one day that she had acquired a new friend named Louise, a physician a few years older than herself, who had recently emigrated from South Africa with her husband.

New bride
Nine weeks before the accident

The two women disclosed their maiden names, and Louise mentioned that when she reported the encounter to her widowed mother back in Cape Town, her mother merely said she had known someone called Glauber many years before. When Barbara told me Louise's maiden name, the penny dropped.

Not long after these conversations, I had an opportunity to meet Louise, who had come up to explore Seattle as a possible permanent home. Remembering that at the time of the accident, on August 31, Eileen had been seven months pregnant, I asked my new acquaintance, "Louise, sorry to be personal when we've only just met, but were you born in Johannesburg at the end of October or in early November 1950?" I don't know how to avoid the cliché, so I have to say her jaw dropped, as she acknowledged the accuracy of my question.

The extraordinary aspect of the event and the reason for telling this story is that Eileen had never disclosed anything about that near-fatal accident to her daughter, a mature woman, a trained physician and a confidante in all matters. I am still puzzled, wondering how deep the feeling of suppressed guilt must have been that even Louise's call to her mother about the name Glauber failed to trigger an opportunity to tell the story or even mention the incident to her daughter. Perhaps the accident that changed our lives had damaged more than one person in that vehicle on that fateful evening.

THE DAY CHRIS CAME TO CALL

Anyone who has undertaken a major life upheaval, as we did in 1980 when we emigrated from South Africa to the United States, will concur that one of the stressful experiences is the process of culling what to take and what to leave behind. Books, artworks certainly, but also matters of sentimental value such as photo albums, theater and concert programs and accumulated magazines.

Two of the latter which definitely made the cut for me were the issue of TIME Magazine of December 15, 1967, autographed by the man on the cover and the South African Medical Journal of December 30, 1967, similarly autographed. The TIME cover story dealt with the first human heart transplant, performed by Dr. Chris Barnard and his team at Groote Schuur hospital in Cape Town, South Africa on December 3, 1967. The heart of a twenty-four-year-old accident victim, Denise Darvall, was successfully transplanted into the ailing body of fifty-four-year-old Louis Washkansky. What has become commonplace throughout the world today obscures the degree of excitement with which heart transplantation was received throughout the world more than fifty years ago. TIME was not alone in highlighting the awe-inspiring story of what seemed the ultimate, the close to impossible surgical miracle. And if worldwide coverage was the norm, imagine, if you will, the excitement in South Africa. After decades of (often but not always deserved) bad publicity, here was a South African achievement to show the country in a most favorable light.

How I came to have my copies signed by the "great man" is the topic of this story. That Barnard and I were both in the medical profession is irrelevant and purely coincidental. Cape Town is 1,000 miles from Johannesburg where I practiced as an anesthesiologist, and there was no reason to expect that our paths would ever cross. I had been an active member of the young men's service organization known as Round Table. I had served in many capacities including the chairmanship of our local Round Table #3 in Johannesburg. Having reached the cut off age of forty earlier in 1967, I was no longer a member of the organization. It transpired that on a certain date in February 1968 my former club was sponsoring a gala screening of the movie *Camelot* as a fundraiser for the South African Heart Association. Somehow, they arranged for the attendance of Chris Barnard who would be passing through Johannesburg en route to a triumphant return to the United States where he had received his training in cardiac surgery. Louis Washkansky had lived only eighteen days with his new heart, but Barnard's second patient, Philip Blaiberg, was by mid-February progressing well enough for Barnard to be able to leave Cape Town. (Dr. Blaiberg eventually survived for nineteen months.) Having secured the presence of Barnard as the added attraction at the gala premiere, ticket prices skyrocketed and now I had my first contact with the project. I received a call asking whether as a fellow medical man I would like to host the distinguished visitor and his wife for one night.

We loved the idea and accepted with alacrity. Then came the logistics of the planned visit. I would meet the Barnards at the airport, bring them home for an early dinner before the four of us headed downtown for the big event. The next order of business, once we had told the children of the possibility that Chris Barnard would be staying with us overnight, was to emphasize to them that it was only a possibility that would become more likely with each passing day. There was always a chance that the condition of the patient might dictate a cancelation of the entire trip. So, kids, you'll just have to do the near-impossible and refrain from telling your friends and classmates. If the visit is canceled, you risk being mercilessly mocked and jeered at for making such an outrageous claim! Next was the question of where would the Barnards sleep? That's easy. They would have our bed, thirteen-year-old Harry would sleep at his friend's next door, and we would move into Harry's room. The girls, fifteen and twelve, would not be disrupted. Nor would four-year-old David. Simple.

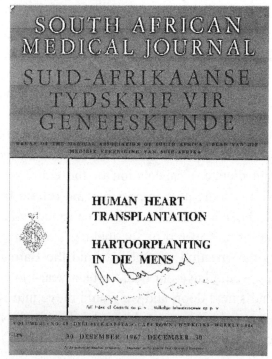

The flight from Cape Town to Johannesburg took place as planned, but when I went to the airport, I was soon reminded that the words of the poet Robert Burns about the best laid plans of mice and men are still relevant. The Barnards had clearly had a mighty argument and the tension was palpable. With barely an acknowledgement of my presence she announced that she had absolutely no intention of coming to Johannesburg but would be taking a cab to nearby Pretoria and would stay overnight with her sister. Clearly this marriage was on the rocks, and indeed after their divorce, the then forty-seven-year-old surgeon was married to a beautiful nineteen-year-old heiress. My guest was in pensive mood for most of the drive home but was cordial and genial on meeting my family. The high point of the brief visit was the photo sessions where he gladly posed with each child in turn, to their utter delight. He ruefully told us that he had better not return to our home after the premiere but would go by cab to Pretoria to try to make peace with his wife. So, on to the highly successful premiere, at which he escorted not Mrs. B but Mrs. G and charmed the audience from the stage. We said farewell and assumed that that was our final contact.

All South Africa followed the news of Chris Barnard's return to his training ground in Minnesota and the veritable explosion of heart transplants being undertaken with varying success in various parts of the world. Several weeks had passed when my receptionist at the office called to say that someone pretending to be Chris Barnard was on the line for me. She and the rest of the staff were agog when I started chatting on a friendly first name basis with the real no-hoaxing Chris. He was briefly in Johannesburg en route to Cape Town and had a proposal he wanted to discuss with me. Could we meet at his hotel the next day? Mystified, and carrying my TIME and my SA Medical Journal for autographing, I set off for our meeting.

At that time, I had established quite a reputation on a very popular radio quiz show. One of several fields in which I had made myself expert was Classical Mythology, and this was the subject of his proposal. Barnard was already at work on his autobiography (published the following year as "One Life"), and would I be willing to write a chapter on the role of the heart in the mythology of different cultures? While greatly flattered and tempted, I gave it long consideration and concluded that I had neither the time nor the research resources (where was Google when you really needed it?) and reluctantly declined.

I had my two precious autographs and that really was the end of my brief tangential contact with the great and famous. Indeed, the only memorable family anecdote remaining from the event concerns our four-year-old son. The day of the anticipated visit was a Tuesday, and on the preceding Sunday morning little David came to our bedroom as usual. Ruth was having her morning tea and reading the Sunday paper, but I had had a grueling night on call and was fast asleep under the bedclothes next to her. David took one look at the huddled hidden body, and remembering that the Barnards were to have our bedroom, asked innocently "Is Chris Barnard here already?"

Were Ruth's raised eyebrows and rolling eyes just amusement at the child's naïveté, or was there a tinge of "if only"?

ON CREATIVITY AND AGING

I have long ridden a hobby horse about the relationship between creativity and aging. I go to a museum and when I have viewed the painting I often read the accompanying description of the work and its history. Automatically, I find myself registering the artist's dates. The pattern I find is quite striking. With obvious exceptions such as suicides (Van Gogh, Pollock, Rothko) or war casualties and victims of tuberculosis (Modigliani) or influenza (Schiele), is it not striking that the vast majority of the great and famous reached extreme old age? A galaxy of artists who by general agreement were among the truly great comes to mind. Picasso (92), Matisse (85), Monet (86), Henry Moore (88), Miro (90), Kokoschka (94), Chagall (98), O'Keeffe (99), Di Chirico (90), Louise Bourgeois (93), De Kooning, Tamayo, Balthus (all 92)…

… the list seems endless.

In the Pacific Northwest, my home for more than thirty years, the so-called Mystic School of painters were cultural icons, not as well known here in California. Morris Graves was the last to die at age 90, predeceased by Guy Anderson (92), Mark Tobey (86) and Kenneth Callahan, a mere 81 years old! Still in the Pacific Northwest, the great married couple of Jacob Lawrence and Gwen Knight left us at ages 83 and 91 respectively. Even in the age of the Renaissance, when life expectancy was so much briefer, we have Leonardo da Vinci living to 67, Michelangelo to 89, Bellini to 82 and Titian to 87 or 88. Raphael, dead at 37, was the rare outlier.

The situation in photography is, if anything, even more striking. Bring to mind the world's most famous photographers and you are confronted with Alfred Eisenstaedt (98), Ansel Adams and Alfred Stieglitz (both 82), Brassai (85), Edward Steichen (94), Andre Kertesz (91), Imogene Cunningham and Berenice Abbott (both 93), and Henri Cartier-Bressler (96). Phew!!

Let me cite just a few literary names, men and women who continued writing well into old age. Doris Lessing died at 94, Toni Morrison at 88, John Barth at 91, while Herman Wouk lived until 104. Tom Wolfe, Philip Roth and Elmore Leonard all lived into their late 80s and at the time of this writing the great Alice Munro is still with us at age 90.

All this, mind you, in the face of the stereotypical perception of the "artist's life"... youthful wild abandon, tobacco and other substance abuse, alcohol aplenty and whatever else makes up the image of a "Bohemian." The further mapping of the human genome will surely one day tell us more about genes and creativity.

When it comes to musicians of genius, my argument is weakened by the tragic deaths in their thirties of such titans as Mozart, Schubert, Chopin and Mendelssohn. Nevertheless, we have Aaron Copland (90), Igor Stravinsky (89), Jean Sibelius (94), Stephen Sondheim (91), Giuseppe Verdi still composing great opera at 80 before dying at 87 and Elliott Carter completing an opera at 96 before dying just weeks before his 104th birthday!

All these voices are sending us a resounding message. That message comes over loud and clear... BE CREATIVE AND DEFY THE AGING BUG!

TAKING THE FIFTH IN TOKYO, 1972

He had always taken great pride in his sense of direction, usually with good reason. He liked nothing more, on arriving in a new city, than to study the map, get his bearings and head out in a chosen direction with complete assurance. And if the alphabet was an unfamiliar one as in Athens back in 1960 or here today in Tokyo twelve years later, well so much greater the challenge and so much greater the satisfaction. Only this morning his wife and the other two had entrusted themselves to his sole stewardship on the train ride to Shinjuku. The intricacies of the Ginza and of the giant department stores presented no problems and they were safely back in the hotel in good time.

But ah, if only his eyesight for the small print matched his confidence in his directional sense, there wouldn't be this story to tell. Although this visual deficiency was the cause of the resulting confusion, it is not the ultimate point of the tale, so nothing will be spoilt by my telling you right now that he had misread the word Tokyu Bunku Kaikan for the more obvious Tokyo Bunku Kaikan... and from that small vowel upset this narrative is born.

Even before the group had arrived in the capital from Kyoto, they had become aware of a forthcoming performance at the Tokyo Bunku Kaikan of Beethoven's Ninth Symphony, that pinnacle of musical creation. Getting tickets via the hotel's concierge was an immediate priority, promptly fulfilled. For both of them, anticipation ran high. They knew that Tokyo boasted no fewer than seven symphony orchestras, more than London or New York.

"I wonder," he said, "how the German words of Schiller's 'Ode to Joy' in the last movement will sound."

"Why should it sound any stranger than the sound of German coming out of English or French or American throats?" she countered.

"True," he conceded, "I just can't wait."

There was certainly an extra frisson of excitement as they prepared to set out for this, their umpteenth Ninth.

The taxi had been summoned, directions on a slip of paper passed from the concierge to the driver who clearly had not a word of English in his vocabulary, and their circuitous route to the concert hall, the Tokyo Bunku Kaikan, began.

Tokyo in 1972 was being well and truly excavated for the expanding subway system. Their hotel stood like a medieval fortress surrounded by a moat of once and future boulevards. It was strange how often they had encountered major road-building upheavals on their travels. They recalled Milan way back in 1960, where the tourist guide joked that the ubiquitous MM signs (for Metro Milano) actually stood for the year that the subway would eventually be completed, maybe! And in Munich in 1966 where you were advised to add an extra half hour to negotiate the torn-up roads to and from the Opera.

So, it was no real surprise to him that the driver—mute, impassive, expressionless—headed east when his map reading had indicated that the hall was just a few blocks northwest of the hotel. But remember that the hall to the northwest was the Tokyu Bunku Kaikan and that the true destination, Tokyo Bunku Kaikan, was indeed to the east, a fact which you, dear reader, know but which the antihero of our story did not.

With the taxi continuing doggedly eastward in increasingly clogged traffic and the driver failing to make any of the obvious left turns to head north, he decided that they were in the hands of someone who didn't know where he was heading, and his notoriously short fuse ignited.

"This guy's lost and we'll never get there."

"Oh relax, or neither of us will enjoy the symphony."

"What do you mean relax—there's not going to be a symphony to enjoy at this rate."

"Please stop spoiling the evening. So we'll get there a bit late."

"A bit late is too late. There's only the one item on the program."

Tensions in the back of the cab were certainly mounting!

At one of the myriad red lights, gesticulating frantically, he showed the driver the tickets and the map but met with a blank stare. And the cab plowed inexorably onward through the dense traffic. As the deadline of 8:00 p.m. neared, it was strange how the back of the driver's close-cropped head came more and more to resemble that of the brutal camp commandant in *The Bridge on the River Kwai*. The mood in the rear had passed from agitation through sighs of resignation to sullen resentment. At which point, with perhaps two minutes to spare, the vehicle rounded a corner to bring the magnificent Tokyo Bunku Kaikan into full view, the last few concertgoers still filing in. With a screech of brakes, they had arrived.

And now the silent driver finally turned round, bared a huge gold-toothed grin, raised two fingers in a Churchillian V-for-Victory sign and in a surprisingly mellifluous voice proclaimed:
DA DA DA DAAAAAH — BEETHOVEN!!

READING FROM RIGHT TO LEFT

A short while ago I was in Paris. More specifically, I was wandering joyfully on the banks of the river Seine. Even more specifically, I was glorying in the atmosphere of the Left Bank, the *Rive Gauche*. And not for the first time I was led to ponder how the innocent French word for "left" has become the far from innocent English word "gauche," implying clumsy, inept, ill-at-ease.

It is a phenomenon in many languages that "left" is not just the opposite of "right" but is inherently inferior. Just as "gauche" has that familiar deprecatory meaning in English, so does the French word *droit* for "right" have its admirable English derivative "adroit," implying skill, accomplishment, capability. Go back to the original Latin words. "Right" in Latin is *dexter*, and we all know how desirable is the attribute of dexterity in any endeavor. The Latin word for left is *sinister*, and is there a less appealing or more threatening word in the English language than sinister?

In German, the word for left, *linkisch,* has come to mean awkward. In Greek, left-handed *skaios* has the connotation of ill-omened. In Mandarin Chinese, the word for left, *zuo*, has come to mean out of accord or improper, and *zuodao* meaning literally "left path" stands for immoral or illegal means. The Yiddish language, too, is particularly rich in its negative allusions to the word for left *linke*. Thus, *linke skheyre* is colloquial for stolen goods. *Linke liebe* connotes an illicit love affair, *linke geld* is counterfeit money, and *oyfshteyn af linke zeyt* means you got up on the wrong side of the bed and all that that implies.

The Bible generally and Christianity in particular are heavily biased towards the right hand. The psalmist calls for the right hand (not the left) to forget her cunning "if I forget thee, O Jerusalem." The right hand of the Lord is exalted, and it is the right hand that doeth valiantly. It is the right hand that makes the sign of the cross, and it is those at Christ's right hand who will inherit the kingdom of God.

The idea that right is simply better than left pervades our language. All's right with the world; we're moving right along; I'll be right with you, all right? You know I'm right.

Contrast all that with the poor folk who have been left behind to chew on leftovers. Who wants to receive a left-handed compliment? Why, the very idea comes out of left field!

The final insult is that those remarkable people blessed with the ability to use both sides equally well are called ambidextrous. The rarely used "ambisinistrous" compounds all that is negative.

Some 80 years ago when my eldest brother was of an age to begin learning to write, his natural left-handedness was subjected to vigorous correction in the mistaken belief that its built-in inferiority would be a lifelong disadvantage. Fortunately, those days are long past, and left-handedness is obviously no handicap in anybody's life. Shed no tears for Ichiro Suzuki and Phil Mickelson, or for Rafael Nadal and John McEnroe! Interestingly, left-handedness seems to be a positive asset in certain highly skilled activities such as computer science. Not only was Alan Turing, the father of computer science, a left-hander but so is Bill Gates and also four of the five designers of the original Macintosh computer. Reputedly one in four NASA astronauts is a lefty, a disproportionately high percentage. And let us not forget that Harry S. Truman, Gerald Ford, Ronald Reagan, Bill Clinton and Barack Obama are just some of the many lefties who made it right to the top!

As a born and bred right-hander, why, you may ask, do I harp on this topic? Could I be a closet lefty? No, perhaps it's because I just want to show my heart's in the right place (on the left). After all, even lefties are covered by the Bill of Rights!

ACCENTUATE THE POSITIVE

When I was a youngster in the 1940s, one of the enduring hit songs was the Johnny Mercer ballad made popular by Bing Crosby and the Andrews Sisters "Ac-Cent -Tchu-Ate The Positive". The lyrics went on to say "Eliminate the Negative". Well, in this complaint of mine about the weird and wonderful usages of the English language I'm not asking for the elimination of the negative, just calling for an even playing field.

Why are there so many examples of the negative in everyday usage? Why shouldn't I be able to say that Sheila's attire is always *shevelled,* that Miranda's appearance is invariably *kempt,* or that the tilt of Gila's cap is at all times just so, completely *wry.*

If my faith in somebody or something proves to be perfectly justified, surely I should be able to express how *illusioned* I am. And if intricate and complicated arrangements work out exactly as planned, I would love to praise everyone involved and tell them how *concerted* I am.

If something really, really great happens (say, at the polls in November) wouldn't we all celebrate in a state of pure, joyful *may*? When things really add up and the problem has vanished into thin air, I claim the right to feel totally *combobulated*. And when you can echo the poet Robert Browning that "all's right with the world" then you should proudly proclaim that you feel truly, truly *gruntled.*

If you believe positively that I have *wittingly* stumbled onto something in the right direction, then join me in shouting out to the world

We will be UPTRODDEN!

SONGS FROM A TRIP TO CHINA

In October 1996, we were part of a group of fourteen who spent a month traveling through China by rail, bus, river boat and airplane. Our various experiences led me to compose new lyrics to some familiar tunes. The first of our several ghastly train rides provoked the following:

> Pardon me boy
> Is that the Xian- Chongqing choo-choo?
> It takes hours twenty-nine
> To reach the end of the line
> You get to use the toilet
> Just a hole in the floor
> Mind the rat poison
> As you slam the door
> Dinner in the diner
> Feel just like a pioneer
> Like no sane American
> Has ever done before

Our tour leader arrived with an upper respiratory infection which he generously shared with all of us, prompting this response:

> Coughing and wheezing and
> Choking and gasping
> Snorting and sneezing and
> Croaking and rasping
> Trying to loosen the mucus that clings
> These are a few of my least fav'rite things

Lots of sore tonsils
And lots of red noses
All sorts of medicines
In increasing doses
How to dispose of
The mucus that clings
These are surely my least fav'rite things

But it's not bronchitis
Or laryngitis
It could be worse
So we don't make a fuss
'Cos we're riding a bus
And not a hearse!
(Yes, the bus was alive with the sound of mucus!)

Of course, there was the inevitable what could be labeled Mao's revenge, and so with apologies to Bernstein's *East Side Story:*

I feel s****y
O so s****y
I feel s****y and c****y, oy veh!
What a pity
What a pity its ten times a day!

Our final train ride before we succeeded in our demand to fly from immaculate airports on immaculate planes elicited this continuation of the original train theme:

When we saw the train
The one that goes Changsha to Guilin
We couldn't restrain
A certain now familiar feeling
If there were paint
You can bet it would be peeling

If there were a fan
You can guess what hit the ceiling
But there's good news, there is good news
Remember it well
We no longer have to use the railroad from Hell
Yes, that was our last night
On locomotive Hades
From now on we sleep tight
Like gentlemen and ladies

And now here is the moral:

My advice could not be finer
Never choose to use choochoos
When next you visit China
Refuse abuse—don't use choochoos
When next you visit China!

BILLINGS COLLECTED; BILLINGS RECOLLECTED

No, this is not a reminiscence of that city in Montana in which I have, in fact, never set foot. Rather, I am recollecting memories of the billing and collection for medical services as practiced in my days as an anesthesiologist in South Africa many years ago.

My partners and I practiced our art in various hospitals around the city. It was not a matter of undervaluing our services... we certainly expected to be paid... but by and large our modus operandi for making that happen was far less aggressive, almost timid in comparison, than is the custom in the USA. This reticence possibly relates to the fact that at that time medicine was still regarded as a noble profession, and that undue emphasis on the financial aspects was somehow inappropriate. We were, after all, physicians and not Provider # such and such in something called the Health Care Industry.

Our practice was, after a polite interval, to send out an initial statement detailing the date and place of service, the name of the surgeon and the nature of the operation performed. In those days many procedures were quite commonly known by the names of the pioneers of that operation. So, for example, a modified radical mastectomy would be named on the statement as a Halsted; varicose vein ligations were shortened to Trendelenburgs, and pelvic floor repairs were Marshall-Marchettis or Fothergills. We had to put a stop to that practice when too many checks would arrive made out to Dr. Halsted, Dr. Trendelenburg or Dr. Fothergill and on one occasion to Drs. Marshall and Marchetti!

A second statement would be sent a month later with the notation "Account Rendered". Only on the third statement would the word "Please" be added. Then, if still unpaid by the fourth month, there would be a polite "This account would appear to have been overlooked. Please remit." Thus, it would be a full five months before the threat of "UNLESS" was rendered. Quite a contrast to the streamlined, no-nonsense business of collecting one's just deserts which I learned on coming to America!

Another feature of medical practice in South Africa was that there was absolutely no way that one doctor would bill for services rendered to a colleague or his immediate family. This professional courtesy was always extended, despite the frequent arguments of many colleagues that they had insurance cover and would rather the bill be paid by the insurance than to have to go to the trouble and expense of buying a gift in appreciation. We would relent on condition that only the insurance amount would be accepted; nothing out of the colleague's pocket. Incidentally, by far the most frequent gift in these circumstances was a bottle of a certain brand of Single Malt Whisky, a tradition so ingrained that one of my partners contemplated marking the label on a bottle rather like a radioactive tracer, just to see how long it took for his bottle to come back to him!

There was another category of patients besides these "pro deo" patients who of course never received a billing statement. It was our custom to extend free services to a remarkably (and indeed ridiculously) wide spectrum of patients including dentists, nurses, physiotherapists and ministers of religion. But in these instances, a single statement of account was sent with the usual details of the service rendered plus a clear two-word message "NO CHARGE".

This worked perfectly in the old days of manual accounting. Now, our practice was one of the first to switch to computerization of our accounts system in the late 1960s or early 70s. You would assume that the task of transferring from primitive manual to sophisticated computerized accounting would be straightforward, but you would assume incorrectly. In Alexander Pope's words, to err is human, but it takes a computer to really... Our computer glitch par excellence affected some of those one-time only NO CHARGE statements. Unbeknownst to us the computer began sending those increasingly pleading and then threatening statements every month all still marked NO CHARGE. Eventually, one patient came to the office, part amused and part angry, waving a sheaf of account statements and begging to be shown how to pay a NO CHARGE fee before being hauled off to court!

My partners and I also owned and operated a freestanding Outpatient Surgical Clinic. The Clinic had its own separate statements for services rendered, detailing the charges for the use of the operating room and for drugs and materials. But for a long time, we were not permitted to charge any fee for the use of the Recovery Room. Eventually the powers that be authorized a Recovery Room Fee— a mere pittance of a few dollars. At that time, we had just had a massive batch of statement forms printed prior to this new allowable fee. Rather than letting this supply go to waste, we authorized our office manager to order a rubber stamp marked "Recovery Room Fee". The minimal space available on the statement form led somebody in the office to shrink the size of the stamp to "Recovery Fee" omitting the word "Room". We realized this when one day a patient came to the office to pay her bill and with a twinkle in her eye teased us with, "You mean that if I hadn't recovered, I could have saved myself five dollars?"

Ah, those were the days!

A SONNET TO A SONNET

Shortly after I joined my writing class in 1998, our instructor challenged us to write a sonnet or a villanelle. With the brashness of youth (I was a mere 71) I decided to tackle both. The opening line of my sonnet refers to what I consider the greatest of any sonnet not written by William Shakespeare. It is Milton's sonnet on his blindness which commences with "When I consider how my light is spent" and concludes with "They also serve who only stand and wait."

When I consider Milton's not my name
And happily today I can record
That being neither blind, nor halt nor lame
Poetic license now I can afford.
Therefore the sonnet form I shall essay,
Not Petrarch- like but homage to the Bard.
Ambition 'tis that drives me in this way
No primrose path this -perilous and hard
First stanza's lines they rhyme a b a b
c d c d's the pattern in the next
e f e f's the rhyme in stanza three
Then g g lines (just two) complete the text.
Success? No way, don't bet upon it
There's more, much more ere it's a sonnet!

A VILLANELLE

The villanelle is a poem of nineteen lines comprised of five 3-line stanzas and a final 4-line stanza. The rhyming pattern is a simple aba. The first and third lines of the opening stanza are repeated in succeeding stanzas, with the opening line becoming the third line of alternating stanzas. They then come together as the final two lines of the poem.

The most famous villanelle in the English language is perhaps Dylan Thomas' "Do not go gentle into that good night" with its concluding line "Rage, rage against the dying of the light." In my cheeky effort I had the effrontery to change the wording of the last two lines, an offense that should have me excommunicated if there were a SPCV... a Society for the Prevention of Cruelty to Villanelles.

The task was set…to write a villanelle
But there's one thing that she would NEVER say
Write not at all if you can't do it well.

Five three-line stanzas with a tale to tell
With simple rhyming pattern a b a
The task was set… to write a villanelle.

The process some would call a living hell
For blest relief they do devoutly pray
Write not at all if you can't do it well.

Will it be said because of pride he fell
Determined to continue come what may
The task was set… to write a villanelle.

Get finished now. I hear the tolling bell
One four-line stanza still stands in the way
Write not at all if you can't do it well.

And now at last it is with pride I swell
Although of course it was more work than play
The task was MET… I wrote that villanelle
Write not at all? Says who I cannot do it well.

WHAT'S THAT YOU WERE SAYING?

In the thirty-two plus years that we lived in Seattle, one of the most (if not *the* most) involving cultural experience was with the Seattle Chamber Music Society. I had attended every single concert since its inception in 1982 and my wife, Evette, served for many years on the Board of Directors in many capacities including the presidency. For the first twenty years or so the annual Summer Festival was held at the prestigious Lakeside School in north Seattle, alma mater of such luminaries as the famous founders of Microsoft and Cellular One. My story today concerns a singular event when building alterations at Lakeside forced that year's festival to relocate to the nearby Shorecrest School. The event to which I refer was much talked about and was mentioned in the concert reviews in both of Seattle's daily newspapers.

Several years later, for the compilation of a celebratory book on the history of the Society and its founder, I recalled the incident in the following lines of verse:

> Of my many memories, one of the best
> Concerns a certain night at Shorecrest
> When there we all sat with our programs before us
> Astonished to hear an unscheduled chorus
>
> That year our tenure at Lakeside had ceased
> Their builders had forced us a mile to the east
> The show must go on... is the Golden Rule
> So, we settled in at Shorecrest School
>
> Our musicians played with their usual feeling
> Until they were joined up there in the ceiling
> By voices that kept getting higher and higher.
> The festival now had a heavenly choir!

Some of us cried "hush", others just said "shoo"
And others just shrugged, what else can you do?
When asked how long they meant to be part of the score
By way of reply they just quoth "Evermore"

One thing I will say for our feathered friends
They sure know how to pursue their own ends
So, let's add to each program the following words,
"Sometimes chamber music really is for the birds!"

Now, the irony of my little poem is that apparently alone among the hundreds there, I actually did not hear a single tweet, chirp or note of birdsong, and I was dissembling madly when joining in all the discussion of the birds in the rooftop. For all this was long before the day when I finally grappled with my failing ability to hear and started the process that led to my acquisition of hearing aids. Like so many others before me, I had resisted, went into a state of denial and found reasons to blame others for not speaking clearly. It was always the inferior cordless phone at fault, never me. My situation was not quite equal to that of my late brother-in-law. He finally acceded to his family's demands that he see his physician. When told by the good doctor to return the following day for a hearing test he arrived with a full specimen bottle. The doctor said "I don't have to test you, my friend. You NEED hearing aids. I told you to come for a hearing test, not a urine test!"

There is something macho about denying the fading of one's hearing that never seems to apply to problems of vision and the correction thereof. Almost everybody wears glasses for some or all daily activities, but somehow many of us feel that hearing aids are an acknowledgment that from here on its downhill all the way. I was even encouraged in denial by my physician who made no bones about his own resolve to avoid auditory "crutches" for as long as possible lest he become increasingly dependent on them.

Over the last twenty years with a succession of increasingly sophisticated hearing aids, a generous supply of batteries and minus several thousand dollars, I have been able to enjoy conversations at a whole new level. I have found film soundtracks to be vastly improved and have gained so much in the pursuit of my favorite cultural hobby, namely listening to music in the concert hall and the opera house. With the newest state of the art hearing aids the use of cellphones does not present a problem. The only negatives are the increased noise levels in crowded situations, even with the program designed to reduce that problem.

I have resisted all blandishments to get smaller, almost invisible aids

I need aids, here they are

I need reading glasses, here they are

I need my cane, here it is

(My answer when asked 'What's with the cane?' is "I'm no longer Abel.")

That is the limited me, the partially disabled me, and I am content.

So, it's time for a toast to my various audiologists over the years, a toast to which I can only echo

HEAR, HEAR!

MATTERS OF GRAVE CONCERN

I have never been particularly attracted to or especially repelled by cemeteries and graveyards. On my travels I have visited the great and famous in places like Highgate in London and Père Lachaise in Paris. And I have been to the graveyard of Trinity Church in Stratford-on-Avon to pay obeisance to you know who.

But a new dimension has been added to my experience. In the early years of this century, I was exposed to the intellectual and emotional experience of visiting some of the World War I graves in Flanders and in France. We made annual visits to Brussels where our son David and his family had been living since 2000, and I became infected with David's enthusiasm and some of his immense knowledge of that conflict.

It was with eager anticipation that he and I set out one weekend in 2002 to visit some of the cemeteries in Flanders and then to the Somme region of Picardy in France. Our first stop was no more than an hour's drive from Brussels, the cemetery of St. Symphorien, a place of pastoral serenity. The grounds are on several levels laid out with rockeries and flower beds like an English country garden. In every direction there was something poignant to observe... the grave of the first Englishman to die in August 1914 not far from that of the last Englishman killed on November 11, 1918. And as though to trump that agonizing misfortune, I saw and photographed the grave of a Canadian soldier killed at 10:58 a.m. on that day, just two minutes before the end of hostilities.

Among the allied gravestones were a sprinkling of German graves, and among the array of crosses in that section were several Stars of David. It was there that we learned that when the Germans again occupied Belgium during World War II, the SS set out to destroy the graves of Jewish German troops of World War I.

Colonel (later Field Marshal) von Mannstein defied Himmler's orders and posted troops to protect the graves of Jewish Germans who had died for their fatherland a quarter century earlier.

World War I graves at Passchendaele Cemetery
Photo by David Glauber

In the Somme one is overwhelmed by the sheer scale of the carnage. The dead are numbered not in the hundreds of thousands but in the millions. There are hundreds of graveyards of varying sizes. On just the first day of the Second Battle of the Somme in July 1916 over 20,000 British troops were killed! I could describe Beaumont Hamel where the entire Newfoundland Regiment was annihilated and where there are still restrictions of movement because of the possible presence of live shells. I could write about Delville Wood where 3,153 South Africans entered the forest to root out the Germans, and on the sixth day only 753 survivors emerged. I

46

could describe Thiepval where a huge (and hideous) memorial bears the names of over 73,000 soldiers who have no known remains or burial place.

Graves containing the remains of individuals uniformly bear only the name and regiment of the deceased, and all too many of them, for lack of identification, bear the words coined by Rudyard Kipling "a soldier known to God."

The scale is so enormous that one attempts to personalize the experience for the sake of perspective. Such an opportunity presented itself on a visit we made in 2003 to Brookwood, the largest Military Cemetery in Britain not far from London. There on a memorial bearing the names of 3500 men and women of the forces "to whom the fortune of war denied a known and honoured grave", David spotted one K E Glauber, a sergeant in the Royal Regiment of Artillery. We began our research. We learned that he was Kurt Erich Glauber, born in Vienna and a resident of Paddington in London where he lived with his parents. He was born in 1902 and had a law doctorate from the University of Vienna. He was clearly part of an Austrian Jewish family that had managed to find an English refuge from Nazi Europe. But we were intrigued. Why would a forty-two-year-old lawyer be serving as a sergeant in the artillery, and how did he die? David's research continued and yielded this fascinating story.

Daniza Ilitsch (born in Belgrade as Danica Ilic) was a famous soprano at the Vienna State Opera from 1936 until 1951. She also sang many roles at the Metropolitan Opera in New York in two seasons immediately after World War ll. She was close to the anti-Nazi underground in Vienna, which almost cost her her life. She and her sister hid a British agent working for the secret service MI6 in their apartment for nearly six months. When the agent was finally arrested in January 1945, the sisters were taken into custody and survived in a camp until Vienna was liberated by the Red Army in April 1945. The agent was not so fortunate and was murdered in Mauthausen Concentration camp in April. He was, of course, Kurt Erich Glauber. His story is rounded off a year later with a War

Office announcement on June 6, 1946, of a posthumous King's commendation for brave conduct.

Our quest for a personal connection based on our fairly uncommon surname was successful, and I only wish I knew what our namesake's spying mission was. In any event, I hope I never become too blasé and too jaded to lose that sense of shock and awe. God forbid that one should ever be unaffected by the horror that is war, any war.

HE'S A POET AND HE DOESN'T KNOW IT

In 2007, in Seattle, my wife and I saw the premiere of an excellent one-man play by the poet David Wagoner. Perhaps I should have used the adjective "first-class" because the play was appropriately entitled *First Class*. The protagonist is the playwright's friend and mentor, Theodore Roethke, the great American poet and charismatic Professor of Poetry at the University of Washington until his death in 1963.

Roethke is expansive on the subject of poetry, imparting new understanding, new insights, new appreciation of sound and structure. He deals with poets past and present, praising some and brilliantly excoriating others. This latter aspect rekindled my own fascination, going back to student days, with the delightful invective of poets on the subject of other poets. I recall the attack on the left-wing poet Stephen Spender:

> *Here simple Spender in a place apart*
> *Bares on his sleeve his hemophilic heart*
> *Dribble by drip the pinkish flow proceeds*
> *Squeeze it, Mr. Spender, thar she bleeds.*

And also about one who shall be nameless:

> *He was so young------------*
> *You mean that by degrees*
> *He might have mellowed into writing "TREES?"*

The South African poet Roy Campbell had a genius for making enemies (he fought for Franco in the Spanish Civil War while many of his contemporaries sided with the "good guys"). Campbell's poem "On Some South African Poets" consists in its entirety of:

You praise their modesty and their restraint
I'm with you there, of course
They use the snaffle and the curb all right
But where's the bloody horse?

But the main thrust of Wagoner's play is Roethke's holding forth to a class of undergraduates (that is of course us, the audience) urging us on the possibilities within each and every one of us to express ourselves as poets.

As one who has dabbled in verse but who has never dared to call himself a poet, I was led to ponder just what makes the difference between a true poet and a versifier or, worse yet, a purveyor of doggerel. Since Pound and Eliot, or even earlier, we have recognized that rhyme and metric rhythm are NOT essentials in modern poetry. How about profundity? For my own meager efforts, I am quite proud of some clever lines and word play, but a lack of depth has made me class myself as a mere occasional writer of verse. My all-time favorite writer of comic verse is Ogden Nash. His gift for creating hilariously witty rhymes (never mind meter) is a joy forever, but he is capable of genuine profundity—a poet, not a versifier. Many of the great and famous have opined on the nature of poetry.

Coleridge defined prose as words in their best order and poetry as the <u>best</u> words in their best order.

Dickens has Sam Weller in *Pickwick Papers* saying, "Poetry's unnatural; no man ever talked poetry."

Samuel Johnson, in reply to Boswell's question, "Sir, what is poetry?" replied "Sir, it is much easier to say what it is not. We all <u>know</u> what light is, but it is not easy to <u>tell</u> what it is."

My own earliest and embarrassing effort arose from an alcohol-fueled undergraduate party a million years ago, "*Glauber ain't sober.*"

More recently I had an amusing experience with the potency of the Internet. In the daily paper of my former hometown of Johannesburg, South Africa, a regular satirical columnist invites readers to submit what he deliberately calls pomes (not poems)—brief little verses with no aspirations to be poetry. On a whim I emailed my *ADVICE TO THE OPERAGOER:*

Avoid those endless restroom lines—
There are always too few loos
Go rather at the place one dines
There's the option you should choose.
What's more, you'll heed those warning signs
To mind your pees...and queues!

Within days, I had not only phone calls from South African friends asking to speak to "the poet" but emails from as far afield as Brisbane and the UK, also addressed to "the poet."

So, thank you to David Wagoner and to Theodore Roethke for making me feel that maybe, just maybe I can say

I'm a poet, and I DO know it.

SAYING HELLO TO THE CELLO

When Mstislav Rostropovich passed away in 2007 a month after his 80th birthday he had long been hailed as the greatest of all cellists. One tribute from a fellow cellist claimed, "he has done more for the cello than any musician has ever done for any instrument." Indeed, he gave the world premieres of well over a hundred compositions. I am among the many millions who respected him enormously, but I had no reason to believe that we would ever meet or that our eventual brief encounter would make this reminiscence worth reporting.

Evette and I usually shun invitations to "meet the artist" receptions. They are overcrowded and the artist frequently looks as though she/he would rather be anywhere else but there fielding fatuous questions after an exhausting evening's work. On an empty stomach yet. But back in December 1998 we were intrigued to receive a written invitation to a sit-down dinner in the Founders Room at Benaroya Hall following the evening's concert given by the Seattle Symphony with Rostropovich as soloist. Although we had been generous donors to the Symphony within our limits, by no stretch of the imagination could we be regarded as major benefactors, and to this day we have no idea why we were included. We accepted, of course, and I knew that in the very remote possibility that we actually got to speak to the great man I already had a topic of conversation in mind.

We had good friends in San Francisco named Sue and Felix Warburg. Felix's father Gerald had been a cellist of professional quality who had his own string quartet and who actually owned all four of the instruments, all Strads. After his death, his cello had come into the possession of Rostropovich and Felix had told me that he was determined to go backstage after his San Francisco concert scheduled two days after the concert in Seattle. So, what a conversation opener I had up my sleeve!

We could hardly believe our good fortune when we gathered in the Founders Room to find that the intimate party was for just 40 people at four tables, and wonder of wonders, we were at the honored guest's table with only the Music Director seated between me and Rostropovich. When the toasts had been drunk and the applause had died down our conversation went something like this:

Me.   Maestro, I have a friend in San…

He.   Not Maestro, you call me Slava

Me.   Thank you, Slava, I have this friend in San Francisco, a man of our age…

He.   What do you mean *our age*, a young fellow like you?

Me.   Slava, I know exactly when you were born, and I'm six weeks older than you. My friend is the son of Gerald Warburg.

He.   Gerry Warburg! A wonderful man. I have his cello. We must drink to him (rising and giving me a great bear hug). And tell your friend he must come and see me after the concert.

For the rest of the evening the conversation focused on his wife Galina Vishnevskaya, the famous soprano who had remained at home in Paris, severely crippled by rheumatoid arthritis. This was the very week that the FDA had given much publicized approval to the new and promising drug Embrel for the treatment of rheumatoid arthritis. Slava was anxious to get hold of the drug immediately. He and his young manager were leaving the next morning for concerts in Portland and then San Francisco. I told them that by pure coincidence we too were going to Portland the next day, not for his concert but to spend the weekend with our physician son Harry and his family. By the end of the evening my mission was clear… try by any means to get hold of as much of the new medication as possible (never mind the cost, whispered one of the zillionaires to me) and deliver it next day in Portland. The manager and I exchanged phone numbers, and Slava graciously signed our program, putting in his own quirkish stamp by Russifying Evette's name to Evettchka.

From then on events moved quickly. Early Friday morning I called my friend David Sabritt whose company manufactured the drug, only to learn from his wife that he was in a meeting in Philadelphia … a blank. A call to my former hospital—yes, it was on the formulary but not yet available… another blank. A call to my son in Portland—Dr. Harry Glauber's hospital didn't even have it on the formulary… blank blank blank. A call from David Sabritt in Philadelphia giving me the contact who might be able to help. Said contact unavailable… blankety blank.

By midafternoon we were on our way to Portland and on arrival at about 6:30 p.m. there was a further message to call Slava's hotel. When I reported my lack of success, the manager graciously offered me two free tickets to the concert. I politely declined but said I would accept four tickets. Then, with Harry staying home with five-year-old Sam, and not bothering with dinner, our daughter-in-law Carole with an excited twelve-year-old grandson Ben in tow made what should have been a thirty-minute drive in twenty minutes and we took our grand circle seats with seconds to spare. Slava was of course wonderful in a program different from the previous evening's offering in Seattle.

Slava had given me his Paris address in case the medication became available later, but I decided not to pursue my chase. I did not feel it was my place to procure a drug about which I knew nothing (oral or injection? refrigerated or not? to be reconstituted or not? Side effects?) to be used by a Paris doctor who would know even less. So there ends the mini saga of Slava and me with just a postscript that the following evening in San Francisco my friend Felix was indeed able to say hello to his father's cello!

Mstislav Rostropovich
CELLO

Internationally recognized as a consummate musician and widely considered to be the world's greatest cellist, Mstislav Rostropovich has recorded virtually the entire cello repertoire and has inspired many of this century's finest composers to create works especially for him. The Chicago Tribune enthusiastically reported after one of his performances that "one goes to hear other cellists play Bach and Beethoven, one goes to a Rostropovich concert to hear Rostropovich...no cellist commands so extensive a tonal range, from a sonorous throb to a ferocious rasp to the most delicate, bell-like harmonics."

Mr. Rostropovich is also a talented and respected conductor and has led many orchestras on every continent. As the music director of the National Symphony Orchestra for 17 seasons, he enjoys special relationships as conductor with such widely varied orchestras as the London Symphony, the Orchestre de Paris and the Vienna Philharmonic.

Mr. Rostropovich has devoted much of his career to the music of the 20th century. With the London Symphony, he dedicated entire performances to the music of Britten, Shostakovich, Prokofiev, and Schnittke. During the 1996-97 season he led concert performances in Moscow and St. Petersburg of Shostakovich's Lady Macbeth of the Mtsensk District, which had not been performed in its original version since 1932. Also because of his interest in contemporary music, he has premiered almost 60 orchestral works, as well as three major operas: Schnittke's Gesualdo and Life with an Idiot, and Shchedrin's Lolita.

Maestro Rostropovich has received more than 40 honorary degrees and over 120 nations have bestowed more than 150 major awards and decorations upon him. Some of these honors include: Knight Commander of the Most Excellent Order of the British Empire, membership in the Academy of Arts of the French Institute, the Presidential Medal of Freedom and a Kennedy Center Honor from the United States.

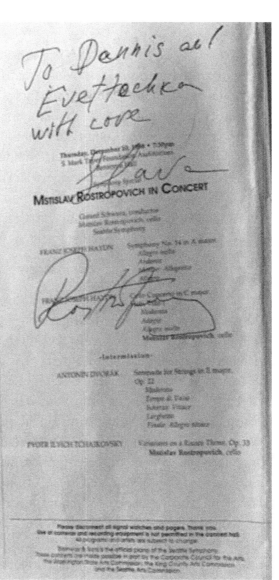

Thursday, December 10, 1998 • 7:30pm
S. Mark Taper Foundation Auditorium

Mstislav Rostropovich in Concert

Gerard Schwarz, conductor
Mstislav Rostropovich, cello
Seattle Symphony

FRANZ JOSEPH HAYDN — Symphony No. 14 in A major
Allegro molto
Andante
Menuet. Allegretto

FRANZ JOSEPH HAYDN — Concerto in C major
Moderato
Adagio
Allegro molto
Mstislav Rostropovich, cello

-Intermission-

ANTONÍN DVOŘÁK — Serenade for Strings in E major,
Op. 22
Moderato
Tempo di Valse
Scherzo. Vivace
Larghetto
Finale. Allegro vivace

PYOTR ILYICH TCHAIKOVSKY — Variations on a Rococo Theme, Op. 33
Mstislav Rostropovich, cello

THAT WONDERFUL WEEKEND

We knew it would be a great weekend, that last weekend of March 2015. All the carefully prepared ingredients were there to satisfy our cultural appetites: a Saturday afternoon symphony concert in Costa Mesa, a theatrical event in Long Beach on Saturday evening, a night in a comfortable Long Beach hotel, Sunday brunch at a venue famous for its Sunday brunches on the waterfront of the Port of Los Angeles, and a Sunday matinee of a much-anticipated contemporary opera in San Pedro, all in the balmiest Californian weather. What was not anticipated, and what turned a great weekend into a wonderful, unforgettable one, is the *raison d'être* of this story.

But first a little background as to why this particular symphony concert on this particular date was so significant to us. In November 1982 my wife Ruth and I were in London attending the conference of the European Society of Anesthesiology. My lifelong dearest friend Sam, a radiologist, and his wife, Evette, were still living in South Africa, from which we had emigrated in 1980. But like so many other physicians at that time, Sam was making active efforts to emigrate and make his medical career in another country.

Quite unbeknownst to us, Sam had come alone to London for job interviews. To our complete surprise, he managed to track us down in that vast city. I absented myself from the conference for the afternoon and also managed to obtain an extra ticket for a private concert that was being given at Royal Festival Hall exclusively for the conference attendees, followed by a fireworks display on the Thames. The performance was by the London Symphony Orchestra and conducted by Michael Tilson Thomas with a brilliant young woman pianist as soloist.

Everything about the evening was a success, and we said a fond farewell to Sam on Waterloo Bridge, not knowing it would be for the last time. A few months later, still in South Africa, at the end of March 1983, Sam collapsed and died suddenly. He was 57. In December of 1984 my wife Ruth passed away in Seattle, aged fifty-six. Since 1986 the widow and widower, Evette and I, have been happily married, and never a day goes by that we don't share happy memories of when there were four of us.

Which brings me back to why the concert that weekend at Segerstrom Hall in Costa Mesa, besides being magnificently played, should have had such profound significance for us. It was, just like thirty-three years earlier, the London Symphony Orchestra conducted by Michael Tilson Thomas with a brilliant young woman pianist as soloist. And the date was the anniversary of the passing of Sam, my dear friend whose memory for me was already indelibly linked with music by the LSO under MTT!

And so on to California State University Long Beach's Carpenter Hall, where British actor Julian Sands presented an evening of Harold Pinter. Pinter was a great playwright who earned the 2005 Nobel Prize for Literature and also earned himself an adjective that has entered the language like Dickens, Shaw, and Kafka before him (Dickensian, Shavian, Kafkaesque, Pinteresque). His prowess as a playwright and polemicist had not prepared us for his achievements as a poet of potency, pungency and wit. Pinter's poetry was the welcome focus of this excellent evening of theater.

Our overnight stay in Long Beach was followed by the promised super brunch on the water. Seating was on the patio with the view of sailing vessels of all sizes: a cruise ship here, a battleship there, and hungry birds everywhere. The convivial spirit at all the tables around us was matched by the quality and, I'm afraid, quantity of the food and drink available.

Time now to move on to the historic Warner Grand Theatre in San Pedro for the performance by Long Beach Opera of a new opera, *Marilyn Forever*. The re-creation of Marilyn Monroe in operatic guise was an inspiration. Two singers conveyed the two aspects of the iconic actress: the spectacular star and the agonized, private and tormented woman. The choice of two different voices, soprano and mezzo, was a brilliant one, and the opera surely deserves wide exposure.

So, three great performances and one great meal. What of the unplanned ingredient that changed great to wonderful? Let me take you back to that brunch on the patio and the prevailing atmosphere of bonhomie. Near us was a large table of African American women, some twenty in number, having a celebration, presumably a birthday. Radiant but never raucous, there was so much joy in the air that people at all the tables could not help but feel part of the celebration.

Next to us was a Hispanic couple with whom we exchanged pleasantries and who were having as much fun as we were. On our other side was a group of three attractive, beautifully dressed African American ladies in their thirties or early forties. I had my back to them, and so my only contact was the exchange of smiles as we passed each other on our repeated trips to and from the brunch tables. But Evette had closer contact as she and they complimented each other on their attire and jewelry. Also, the one lady was very attentive in assisting Evette, who had her right arm in a sling following recent surgery.

We had raised our champagne glasses repeatedly as we toasted ourselves and our alter egos, Sam and Ruth. Our waiter had been assiduously pouring the champagne for us all morning but by the end of the meal was nowhere to be seen. When I finally hailed him and asked for our check, he stunned me by saying our bill and gratuity had already been paid! The "fairy godmother" was the young lady from the next table who had been so attentive to Evette.

Overcome and astonished, we asked her WHY? And I paraphrase her reply. She said she had had a rough life, which she hoped would at last turn the corner with her upcoming marriage. She loved her boyfriend but was full of trepidation about how it would turn out. Observing us and our evident joy in each other's company, she just prayed that she could find such happiness when she reached our age. Paying for our meal would be recompense for providing that hope and would make a fine start in fulfilling her dream. From then on, it was hugs and kisses and all five of us on the brink of tears.

"Goodness gracious" is an exclamation that has perhaps become a cliché, but this was goodness and graciousness personified. We felt both proud and privileged to live in a society that nurtures such qualities. To round off this wonderful weekend, we resolved to pass on the goodness with a generous donation to whichever of the various good causes would have an appeal in the next day's mail, for there would surely be at least one. And there was. And we did.

TENNIS, ANYONE?

When I was growing up in South Africa, sport—either as a participant or as a spectator—was a major part of one's life. I imagine it was the same for you, dear reader. When it came to team sports at school, the so-called pinnacle of my achievement was a place on the school's Under-13 B Football (soccer) team where I distinguished myself not at all. Nevertheless, I managed to insinuate myself into the front row for the official team photo, holding the ball yet!

As a spectator, I identified with a particular First Division team called the Germiston Callies (for Caledonians), and to this day more than eighty years later I can remember the names of three of their key players. And nothing would prevent me from attending their games wearing a shirt that exactly matched their maroon uniforms. Then at about the age of ten or eleven, I converted to the South African religion known as Rugby Football, and although I followed the game assiduously and can reel off the names of bygone stars, I do not recall any passionate identification with a particular team.

But it isn't team sports which continue to fascinate me, but rather the one on one of individual contests. And with due respect for such endeavors as squash, badminton or racquetball, nothing ranks with tennis or golf. Golf is in part a contest between the player and the course, and only tennis provides the pleasure of a pure mano a mano contest to see who is the superior one. My wife, Evette, had a similar upbringing, although she was far more adept at sports like field hockey and golf.

So, our house is occupied by two genuine tennis nuts. In South Africa it was not unusual for private homes to have a tennis court, and ours was in use several days of the week, and for our men's group Saturday afternoon was sacrosanct, weather permitting, which meant about forty-eight weeks of the year. It is difficult to exaggerate the sheer pleasure that Saturday tennis provided eight enthusiastic but mediocre players at the end of a stressful week. The standard of play didn't matter; the fun was in the feeble jokes which somehow got funnier with repetition. I recall Issy who frequently displayed what he called his specialty shot and would then proceed to spell it out loud M I... SHIT. I fondly remember Arkie who tried to persuade us that foot faults and double bounces didn't really count, and who would inspect the line in a disputed close call and then with a preposterous fake German accent would pronounce "Claus, aber aus" (Close, but out.) And my dearest friend Sam who one day, when the set was clearly drawing to a close, called to the group waiting to go on court next, "Gentlemen, you may gird your loins." After that gem was repeated a few dozen times it was abbreviated to "gird your loins" and eventually just "girdle". It was Sam of course who took that to its logical conclusion by calling "girdle" earlier and earlier in the match, culminating in a call after somehow winning the first point of the first game of the set. Tennis nuts indeed, but what lasting joy the game provided.

Then there was the series of annual Wimbledon parties. In Seattle, every year for about twenty years we hosted a party on the first Sunday in July timed to coincide with the Gentlemen's Singles Final. No problem that the match is televised live and that the starting time of 2:00 p.m. in London is 6:00 a.m. on the West Coast. Promptly at 5:55 a.m., up to sixteen bleary-eyed tennis fans were at our door, $5.00 in hand ready to place their bet on the result. Obviously, there can be only one winner and one loser so the wager had to forecast how many sets, and if there was an overlap in predictions we required a prediction of the score of the deciding set, the most accurate prediction scooping the pool. The finances having been dealt with, the party could proceed. By 7:00 a.m. the champagne was flowing, the cucumber sandwiches were devoured and the strawberries and cream were in the offing. Who needs to face the endless lines and the milling crowds of a real trip to Wimbledon?

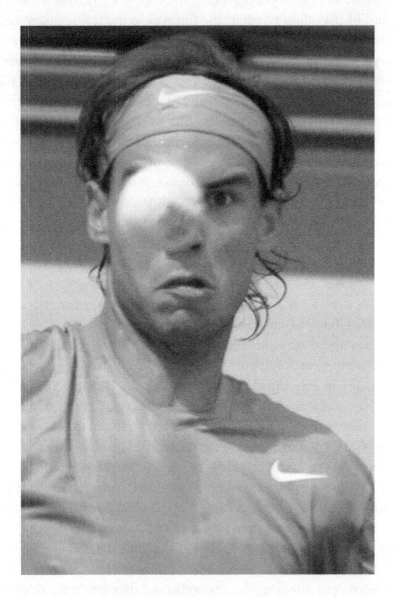

Rafael Nadal at Roland Garros
Photo by David Glauber

I come now to the question of Evette's romantic entanglements with certain players. For many years her obsession with Pete Sampras was widely known to everybody but Pete Sampras. She couldn't bear to actually watch the match in case she put him off his stride! When he won the title, which he did seven times, she would get congratulatory international calls and e-mails, and when Pete married the lovely actress who is now Mrs. Sampras, Evette got a call from a dear friend in Texas saying "Is he out of his mind? Why do this when he's got you?"

Once at Indian Wells at the practice courts I managed to get a photo of Pete when he was crossing the court and appeared to be in close juxtaposition to Evette. For a while, that framed photo displaced all the grandkids' pictures. But all things come to an end, and Sampras was replaced in Evette's affections by the great Roger Federer (eight Wimbledon titles and counting).

Latest reports are that the Federer marriage has survived.

I have always had great respect (with one exception) for the subeditors or copy editors who compile witty headlines that stick in the memory. Nowhere is this better illustrated for me than the local newspaper at Indian Wells in the Coachella Valley. The annual tournament at Indian Wells is the biggest in the world after the four Majors and we have been fortunate to have attended regularly for several years. The Desert Sun publishes a huge supplement each day devoted to the tournament at the Tennis Garden, as the facility is officially called. I admired the subeditor's headline a few years ago when the top ranked woman was surprisingly beaten. It read "First Seed planted in the Garden."

On another occasion, when the great Roger Federer met the identical fate, the headline was in faux military style "Roger, over and out." I'm sure that somewhere there's an editor waiting to label the sensational teenager Carlos Alcaraz with something like "They're ALL CARAZY about Carlos." I haven't actually seen such a headline, but remember you saw it here first.

I mentioned earlier the exception in my overall respect for headline writers. Here's why. In 1971, I attended as usual the

Ladies' Singles Final at the South African Open in Johannesburg. The title holder and overwhelming favorite was the top-seeded great Billie Jean King. But she was surprisingly upset by the Australian star Margaret Court. As soon as the match was over, I headed all the way downtown to the office of the Sunday Times with a note for the subeditor, saying "Here's your headline for the sports section tomorrow." It read COURT QUEEN CHECKMATES KING.

Needless to add, they didn't use it. Who says you can't nurse a grudge for fifty years?

REFLECTIONS ON AGE AND AGING

I have always believed that a birth certificate is actually a two-part document, of which the second part is the date of death, patiently awaiting an undetermined date to be filled in. Intrinsic to that concept is the belief that the aging process commences on Day 1. The transitions from infancy to babyhood to toddler status are landmarks of delight, bringing smiles to proud parents and even prouder and boastful grandparents. But they can be viewed as just further notches in the aging process. It is all, as they say, a matter of perspective.

The day the traffic cop who pulled you over looks more like a schoolboy than an ogre is another landmark in perspective. When I was still working in the operating rooms, one of my younger colleagues "celebrated" her attainment of reaching the advanced age of (whisper it) BIG 4-0 by being wheeled in on a gurney whose IV pole was festooned not with a bag of fluid but with four black balloons. From my present nonagenarian viewpoint, that seems as ludicrous as it is amusing.

For me, a memorable perspective was set when, as a twenty-three-year-old about to marry my twenty-one-year-old fiancée, I was involved in the delicate family discussion of wedding invitations. My prospective father-in-law insisted that a certain business acquaintance had to be included as "I've known him for twenty-five years." Ruth and I exchanged glances and rolled eyes with the unspoken comment:

"Good Lord, he's talking about a quarter of a century!"—an unfathomable period.

It is a truism that middle age keeps retreating just as you approach it, and we all repeat the old adage that you are only as old (or as young) as you feel. I like to joke that when at last you are reconciled to the fact that you are approaching middle age, it is extremely disconcerting to find your kids there waiting for you!

So, what is the perspective at age ninety-five? Is it time to sit back (or lie back) and enjoy the benefits and the handicaps that one has earned over so many years? I must say that I continue to believe that as long as you still want to learn, as long as you are still eager to be surprised by a new discovery, you are not old.

We had the privilege of knowing the late Jerry Binder Ph.D. as a lecturer in psychology, philosophy and history as well as a raconteur and finally as a good friend. He devoted his last years to what he called a "fountain of age", recognizing that aging involves loss and decrement but that it also deeply enriches. I stress that the beautifully expressed sentiments below are his words, not mine. He urges us to refuse to be self-absorbed in a "D" life; endlessly talking about disability, disease, death, depression, dementia, decay, doldrums, deterioration. In the "D" life our heart song is a dirge. He calls on us to join the "A-Team": Celebrate being active, alert, amiable, able, animated, astute, attractive, amazing, apt, awesome, artistic, adventurous, affable, ambitious, admirable, aware, accomplished, affirming, avid, authentic, and—yes!—alluring, adorable and amorous! On the "A-Team" our heart song is an anthem!

Bravo to that, dear Jerry.

A GUIDE FOR THE PERPLEXED TRAVELER

The title of this essay is a tip of the hat to the great medieval thinker, philosopher and physician Maimonides whose masterwork is his *Guide for the Perplexed.* Recent conversations with two different friends were disturbing, as each expressed the dismal thought that their traveling days were now over. Having been fortunate to have traveled extensively over the decades, I felt encouraged by the feeling that for me the next journey to far off parts is still exciting and still within the bounds of possibility, at least physically if not fiscally. In that regard, dare I add that "Maimonides days doesn't go as far as it used to." Ouch!

Besides the fairly regular visits that Evette and I make to family in the UK and Europe, we have been to the Far East and Australasia more than once, and in earlier days my wife Ruth and I were able to make the grand tour of Europe for a three-month period on two occasions in the 1960s, the latter including our first ever visit to the US. So the memories are abundant. When I reflect on the highlights of so much travel, I am intrigued by how so many memories hinge on tour guides. For example, while I recall many other highlights of our first visit to Copenhagen in 1960 (the Tivoli Gardens, the Little Mermaid, the palaces), it is our guide's introductory quip that "Danish isn't a language; it's an affliction of the throat" that stands out. When I think about our visit to Milan that same year, I naturally treasure having seen Leonardo's Last Supper and having visited La Scala (no performance, alas) and the great cathedral where building began about eight centuries ago and is still underway. But what comes to mind most vividly is a delightful quip by our tour guide. Milan in 1960 was chaotic, the main streets being dug up for the building of the subway system, a project that had obviously been underway for several years. Everywhere were the signs showing MM... obviously standing for Metro Milano. But our guide wryly added that the letters really stood for the year construction would actually be finished… maybe!

Another occasion when the guide provided the best remembered experience was when Evette and I were back in a South African Game Reserve, a regular haunt in our past days but now for the first time as American tourists. We crowded together with a horde of young Germans to listen to the words of the young lady who was our ranger/guide, "You may be wondering why I carry this rifle. You must understand that these animals are DANGEROUS, so if you try to leave the vehicle when we make our stops, I'm going to have to shoot you!"

In Moscow, high up among the many memories is the tour of some of the stations in the vast Metro subway system. Many are artistic masterpieces which we are so glad to have visited, but what sticks in the memory is our guide Violeta's warning: "There are 231 stations in the system and if you don't stay close and keep your eyes on me you could land up seeing every single one."

When Evette and I returned from Alaska to Seattle on our honeymoon in 1986, we traveled on a vessel of the Princess Line. The passengers were assembled for a general briefing by the purser. I still remember him saying "This a British vessel and as you can see from the insignia on our uniforms all the officers are British. But when you go down for dinner you will observe that all the kitchen and dining room staff are Italian" and then with a pause and exquisite timing born of repetition he added "Aren't you glad it isn't the other way round?"

Our trip to Ireland in 2015 provided the most remarkable guide that I have ever experienced, a true performance artist. In the town of Mullingar our group of nine assembled to meet our guide, a young man named Paul who introduced himself and then apologized that he had been called away and would hand us over to the care of a substitute called Mary who would, he assured us, be more than competent in his place. When Mary led us to a square where a statue commemorates the site where James Joyce wrote part of *Ulysses,* a lone middle-aged man, waistcoated in early twentieth century garb was sitting on the steps reading a book. He began to interrupt and heckle poor Mary. He soon took over and for several minutes lectured on Joyce as though he were the great writer himself. Despite the age disparity, he looked a bit like our departed guide Paul. A puzzlement!

Further on the tour, Mary was discoursing on the historic old courthouse when she was rudely interrupted by a blue-bereted uniformed soldier who took over the story. Obviously, Paul again in yet another disguise. Before the afternoon was over, Mary's disquisition outside the Protestant cathedral was completely disrupted by the dumb show antics of a crazed hooded Franciscan monk who was of course Paul yet again. We learnt so much from this remarkable guide who later that evening joined us at the hotel and entertained us further with his own beautiful poetry. A different Irish guide was memorable for his contention that guiding around Killarney was as easy as A B C… **A**nother **B**loody **C**astle!

But my favorite memory regarding tour guides remains our experience of visiting the Carmelite Monastery on Mt. Carmel in Haifa in 1960. It was a fascinating and informative tour given by one of the monks. In typical brown robes and monk's tonsure he could have sprung from a painting by Giotto or Raphael. He spoke excellent English in what we both recognized as a South African accent. So, at the end of the tour I asked him about his background, about which he was only too eager to talk. Yes, he was South African, a nice Jewish boy from Cape Town named Jack Friedman who had graduated in Medicine about ten years before I did. It is to this day a surreal experience to recall how we exchanged reminiscences…

Did you know so-and-so?

Of course, we were in the same class

And what's-his-name?

Sure, we were after the same girl, but he won.

This bizarre conversation continued deep in the bowels of a famous and profoundly Christian landmark. I regret that I never did find out how and why why **WHY** did Dr. Jack Friedman become Brother Elias in a monastery thousands of miles and many light years away from his roots. In this regard it was I who was the perplexed traveler in need of yet another guide.

CONSIDERED TRIFLES

I ask myself whether it is really justifiable to compose an entire essay leading to the recounting of a mere witticism (not mine, but I wish it had been). Considering the remarkable coincidences involved, I do believe it is a tale worth telling, so please bear with me.

Highlights of every summer with us have always included participation in UCI's New Swan Theatre's Shakespeare Festival. Each year a comedy and a tragedy are staged over several weeks, and on one weekend in August workshops are held involving interactions with directors and cast as well as lectures from local and outside experts, followed by the evening performance.

In August 2018 one of the chosen plays was *The Winter's Tale,* an estimable work with insights into male paranoia, female forgiveness and much else besides. Now, if you say the word *Hamlet,* a hundred quotations come to mind, with "to be or not to be" leading the pack; say *Macbeth* and it's "tomorrow and tomorrow and tomorrow" or "all the perfumes of Arabia"; *Richard III*—who can forget "the winter of our discontent" and from *The Taming of the Shrew* "Kiss me Kate" springs immediately from one's lips. *The Winter's Tale* is, for me, not that rich in quotable material, but the one line that stands out is when the character Autolycus, a thief, a charming rogue and a thoroughly likeable con man, calls himself **a snapper-up of unconsidered trifles**, a job description as vivid as any set down by the Bard or by anyone else.

So, we had attended a technical rehearsal, the all-day workshop, the performance, and for good measure a further workshop a few days later devoted to the songs and music in this and other plays.

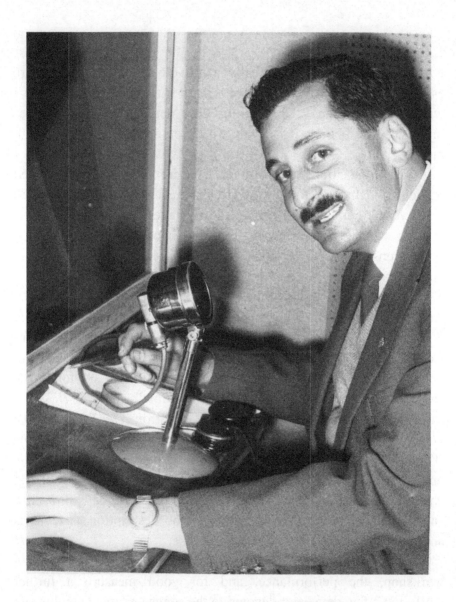

In the studio considering trifles

Immediately after this last exposure to the play and its memorable snapper-up of unconsidered trifles, Evette and I set off for La Jolla and its Summerfest Music Festival. We usually listen to books or music on CD during long drives, but at that point we had just the one old car which boasted only a cassette player, no CDs. But wait— somewhere in a closet in the garage I had a box of old cassettes which we grabbed and threw onto the back seat.

Where is this heading, you ask. Be patient, say I.

Back in my native South Africa, I had acquired a certain degree of prominence as a contestant on the radio quiz show '21' appearing intermittently throughout the 1960s and into the 70s. The highlight of the entire series was the creation of '21 International' in 1968. I had outlasted the opposition to earn the right to represent South Africa against contestants from four other countries. From the US came the then-biggest prize winner on Jeopardy. The UK sent the current BBC Brain of Britain, and other worthies came from Ireland and from South Africa's neighbor Zimbabwe, then called Rhodesia.

For an intense week we recorded three or four half-hour shows every evening for later weekly broadcast. When the battles were finally over (modesty prevents me from saying who won), there was time to record a friendly nothing-at-stake contest of North v. South. The three Northerners were dispatched to another studio while I and my Rhodesian erstwhile rival/now partner (a delightful gentleman named Hugh Finn) squeezed into one of the soundproof, viewproof, airproof booths designed for one, ready to do lighthearted battle with the North.

All this I remembered from fifty long years previously, but of course details of actual questions had long been forgotten. Back now to our drive down the I-5 to La Jolla. Evette pulled out a cassette at random which turned out to be a tape of this friendly N v. S contest. I had not heard it for fifty years and Evette had not heard it at all. So how weird it was that less than an hour after being steeped in *The Winter's Tale* we were listening to the following taped exchange.

The question was: - Since its construction to the present time, how many people have leapt from the Eiffel Tower to their deaths? Naturally, neither of us had a clue to the answer to this esoteric question, but like many a veteran quiz contestant, I had memorized many other facts about the Tower which I was not going to allow to go to waste. So, I began to banter lightheartedly with the quizmaster:

"Are you referring to the one named after Alexandre Gustave Eiffel?"

"Yes, that one." (audience laughter)

"You mean the one that took two years and two months to build and opened in 1889?" (more laughter)

"Yes, that one and please answer the question."

"You mean the Eiffel Tower that's 1,063 feet high and has 2,500,000 iron rivets?" (even more laughter)

And then, ever so gently, my hitherto silent friend Hugh asked: "Is the person assigned to remove the bodies a snapper-up of unconsidered **Eiffels**?" (uproarious cheers and laughter)

Legend has it that Oscar Wilde once said about a particular *bon mot* "I wish I had said that", to which the painter James Whistler responded, "You will, Oscar, you will."

Now, thanks to William Shakespeare and Hugh Finn I can say "You did, Dennis, you did."

R.I.P. NA2SO4

In April 2018, we had a death in the family. The dear departed was just twenty years old, but hold your tears at this apparent premature loss, because she had traveled widely and had well over 240,000 miles under her fan belt. Yes, it was my beloved red 1998 Subaru Legacy that had succumbed—a sudden heart attack manifested as a shattered camshaft. And the event took place without warning on Moulton Parkway at the corner of Ridge Route, right outside the DMV. There's an ironic setting worthy of Chandler's Philip Marlowe or Hammett's Sam Spade—a DoA at the door of the DoT.

With the demise of the Subaru came the decommissioning of my personalized license plate that I have had on all my vehicles since coming to the USA in 1980—NA2SO4.

Na2SO4 is the chemical formula for Sodium Sulfate. Sodium Sulfate is also known as Glauber's Salt. Johann Rudolf Glauber was a seventeenth-century Dutch/German alchemist. I highly doubt any kinship between J R Glauber and my family. Glauber discovered Sodium Sulfate in 1625 and called it *sal mirabilis.*

Glauber's Salt is widely known throughout the world for its principal use as a laxative similar to its close cousin Magnesium Sulfate (Epsom Salts). When I was growing up in South Africa, the product, though close to obsolescence, was well known, and my brothers and I all had to endure the schoolboy nickname of Salts or Zaltz. So, it came as a surprise to me how little known it was in this country. I responded to innumerable queries from fellow motorists, pedestrians, bus drivers and once even a traffic cop who pulled me over just to ask what my plate meant. Seldom did my explanation ring a bell. Few of my medical colleagues, with presumably some chemistry tuition in their training, had ever heard of it.

Some years ago, our annual trips to Santa Fe triggered a desire to commission a tapestry that would reflect the multiple shades of red in the New Mexican desert. We sought several bids in Santa Fe and then went out to Taos Pueblo to see the work of a highly recommended weaver. We found her in a most unprepossessing dimly lit backyard workshop, admired what we saw and asked her to submit a bid. When I began to spell my name, I had reached the third or fourth letter, when she interrupted with:

"You mean the same as Glauber's Salt?"

We both hugged her with delight and expressed our surprise when she explained that it is used every day in textile dyeing. She got the contract, the tapestry is gorgeous and has never faded, and I now know that NA2SO4 did not perish with the Subaru. On the contrary, it lives on and is something to dye for!

Evette at NA2SO4's last resting place

ON REREADING THE GRAPES OF WRATH

Some years ago, my study group in Seattle devoted an entire semester to John Steinbeck's great novel *The Grapes of Wrath*. In addition to reading the book we were exposed to the music of the era, notably that of Woody Guthrie, inspected artefacts made by participants in the events of the 1930s and shown to us by their descendants, viewed the classic John Ford movie (1940) and saw a stage play based on the novel.

The storyline is too well known to require a detailed outline. Suffice it to say that in this almost biblical saga to the promised land of California, the Joad family and their cohorts encounter just about every hostile assault that humankind in the form of harsh authority, resentment and greed can inflict, compounded by the natural devastations of drought and flood.

There are several themes developed in the novel. One is epitomized by Ma Joad's final speech to the effect that "We are the people, and the people will go on. The rich will come and go but we cannot be crushed and will not disappear. We are the people." There is also her son Tom's pronouncement when he, having killed a man, must for the good of the family strike out on his own. When his mother despairs that she will never see him again and will not know what is happening to him, he assures her that he will be everywhere... wherever an underdog is fighting for survival, he'll be there.

At about this time my attention was drawn to the words of the great Chilean poet Pablo Neruda. He recollected that it was as a small child that he first conceived a precious idea... *that all of humanity is somehow together*. And this resonates with the most central theme of Steinbeck's novel, delivered by the former preacher Jim Casy. He can preach no more because he has lost the spirit. A preacher, he tells Tom, has to know, and he doesn't know; he can only keep asking. Several times in the novel Casy, pre-echoing Neruda, opines that each man's spirit is just part of a greater spirit... *Maybe all men got one big soul ever 'body's a part of.*

Of course, much the same idea was wonderfully expressed three centuries earlier by John Donne in his epic lines:

> *No man is an island entire of itself....any man's death*
> *diminishes me because I am involved in mankind; and*
> *therefore never send to know for whom the bell tolls; it*
> *tolls for thee.*

Much of the heartbreak of the book is heightened by our present awareness of the plight of later sets of migrants fleeing disaster... driven from their homes not by the dust and drought of the 1930s but by the hurricanes and floods of 2005, 2017, this year and probably the next, and of course those fleeing death and destruction in the carnage of war-torn Syria and the chaos of turbulent Central America.

One can only hope that the newest homeless will find a more receptive and compassionate America than did their Dustbowl predecessors.

So sharp was the contrast between the reception given the migrants in *The Grapes of Wrath* and the noble words of Emma Lazarus enshrined at the base of the Statue of Liberty, that I was moved to put the following thoughts into verse:

On Reading *The Grapes of Wrath*
or
"The Statue of What?"

The huddled masses who yearned to breathe free
How lucky they were that they came o'er the sea
Had they made the arduous journey by road
They'd have met the grim fate of the family Joad.

It was "okay".. You're in, come unburden your load
And not "okie".. You're out, for the likes of Tom Joad
California made clear, and their methods were cruel
From the slashing of wages to the high price of fuel.

From the beatings and cheatings and swung baseball bat
Slim pickings, knife stickings and the unwelcome mat
If you're poor you're a threat so understand that you
Just don't meet the criteria on Liberty's statue.

But history rolled on as we all know it must
The country survived that dread bowl of dust
And one thing is clear as the story unfolds
This time it is Steinbeck for whom NOBEL tolls!

SHOTS IN THE DARK

As I write these lines in the final days of this *annus horribilis 2020*, the whole world has been engaged in a once-in-a-century crisis—the battle of the V's. On one side the virus, vicious and villainous; on the other the now viable, valiant and (deo volente) victorious vaccine. Not surprisingly, my thoughts have gone back to a previous time when the world grappled with and conquered a dread disease. My very peripheral association with Jonas Salk and the poliomyelitis vaccine is the topic of this tale.

Johannesburg, the largest city in South Africa, is where I grew up and went to Medical School. About an hour's drive away lies the town of Vereeniging on the banks of the Vaal River. This was the historic place where the Peace Conference ending the Anglo-Boer War (1899-1902) took place. We used to joke that the only redeeming virtue of living in Vereeniging was that it was only an hour away from Johannesburg. In the period immediately following World War II, a new town sprang up some ten miles downriver from Vereeniging, a steel manufacturing city called Vanderbijlpark. It was there that I set up medical practice in April 1952. The in-joke was extended so that when asked how I could banish myself to such a cultural wilderness, I could reply that, after all, it's only fifteen minutes away from Vereeniging!

No sooner had my pregnant wife and I ensconced ourselves in the local hotel and begun establishing a practice and a search for permanent housing, when a stroke of rare good fortune came my way, my first contact with Americans en masse. This was the arrival of the first few of what soon became dozens of many young families from the USA. They were engineers from the MW Kellogg Company, here to establish the world's first plant for the extraction of oil from coal. South Africa is cursed by a dearth of oil reserves and blessed by an abundance of coal, much of it in incredibly rich seams just on the other side of the river opposite Vanderbijlpark. So that was to be the site of a new entity SASOL and a new city Sasolburg. And it was my good fortune that the first question the young American mothers had for the hotel management was the whereabouts of the nearest medical practitioner. The answer obviously was Dr. Glauber right here in the hotel.

There was no bridge over the river at this early stage. Transport of all dimensions was achieved, believe it or not, by a pontoon ferry operated by a pulley system powered by donkeys! All this rapidly changed as the huge new plant and city grew and sprawled across the countryside. Now the joke was further extended, and we consoled the prospective residents of Sasolburg that, after all, they were only twenty minutes away from Vanderbijlpark! My American practice grew apace; babies were delivered; firm friendships were made. Remote places that I had never heard of like Casper WY, Allentown PA and Waco TX became real and familiar as though I had been there personally.

And then came the miracle of the Salk vaccine. Jonas Salk and his Pittsburgh team had worked for many years on developing a safe and effective vaccine, funded in large part by the March of Dimes, a grass roots nationwide movement inspired and led by the most famous of all polio victims, the late president Franklin D Roosevelt. Fittingly, the triumphant announcement came on April 12, 1955, ten years to the day after FDR's death. I should mention that during the severe polio epidemics of 1952 and 1953 prior to the existence of a vaccine, we sometimes used a stopgap preparation called gamma globulin. This had no specific relation to the three types of polio virus, and at best might have given passive immunity lasting barely five weeks. Its main benefit would have been in allaying the fears of panicky parents. Perhaps I need to remind younger readers that such panic and terror, summer after summer, was widespread and fully justified, such was the devastation caused by poliomyelitis.

When the Salk vaccine was released in the USA, it was also licensed for production in research centers around the world. The Poliomyelitis Research Foundation of the South African Institute for

Medical Research was authorized to mass produce the vaccine strictly according to the Salk protocol, and supplies became freely available. One day several of my American patients/friends approached me as a group with the news that they had ordered and arranged the delivery of Salk vaccine to be flown out from the USA specifically for their use. Their understanding (a completely erroneous one) was that the South African vaccine was to be restricted only to South African citizens. In retrospect, I think they felt that the local product would be inferior to the "real thing" from the USA, and they had contrived a tactful way to get around this potentially embarrassing quandary.

Came the big day when the consignment was due to arrive and I was invited to accompany my friends to take delivery at the airport, some fifty miles away. Once back in my office, I opened the precious carton to find vial after vial, bottle after bottle of gamma globulin!!! I gently chided my friends for venturing out of their own fields of expertise into the dark and spending a fortune on a product of which they knew all too little. The upshot was that they and their families, like the rest of us, had their shots the South African way, with total success. And I was stuck with a refrigerator loaded with expensive gamma globulin awaiting suitable indications for its use.

From this distance of sixty-five years, I'm afraid I don't recall which came first... the expiry date of the product or my wife's ultimatum to get that stuff out of her fridge or else!

WHAT'S IN A NAME?

The name of the street where we live in Laguna Woods Village is Paseo del Lago. We love our home and its congenial surroundings, and it is an additional bonus to have a street address which is so euphonious and even exotic. For the preceding twenty-five years we lived in our beautiful home in Seattle at 3556 NE 147th Street, an address about as enchantingly evocative as, say, our son's address in Portland at 7247 SW 29th Avenue. BORING! I appreciate that in large cities a numerical system does at least give people a pretty clear idea of where to find any given address. Nevertheless, I do miss the fascinating allusions and educational opportunities that the street names provided in the various places in which I lived in my native South Africa.

The city where I was born is called Benoni, named incidentally for a biblical reference to Ben-Oni, "son of my sorrow." Benoni had been largely developed by an early gold mining magnate who hailed from Bedfordshire in England. The house where my brothers and I were born was in Woburn Avenue, named for Woburn Abbey, still today the seat of the Duke of Bedford (take that, Downton!). Neighboring streets like Cranbourne and Howard were also redolent of the founder's antecedents, and to me are very pleasing and stimulating.

The streets of Parkview, the neighborhood where I lived immediately after my marriage, are all named after counties in Ireland. Is there a better way to conjure up and to dream of a visit to foreign parts than to live on the corner of Tyrone and Roscommon, not far from Dundalk? Or go to the adjoining neighborhood of Parkwood, where the counties that make up Wales all provide the delightful prospect of a walk from Swansea to Glamorgan. To the inquiring mind, how much more seductive than NE 147th!

But the best example that this exercise in nostalgia provides is the town of Vanderbijlpark, where I set up medical practice as a twenty-five-year-old back in 1952. This was a brand-new city, laid out immediately after World War II as the home of a major iron and steel center. The principles of town planning then were to avoid the grid of innumerable cross streets and to develop separate neighborhoods, each with its own shopping center and hardly a straight street or avenue to be seen.

The city was based on several major broad boulevards named Curie, Einstein, Newton and Faraday. Each of the self-contained neighborhoods branching off the main boulevards had streets dedicated to a particular field. So, the Shakespeare Street shops were surrounded by houses on Dickens, Milton, Wordsworth and Longfellow. Go to the Edison shops and find yourself walking on deForest, Fresnel and Bessemer Streets. On Sundays my wife's parents and my teenage sister-in-law would come out from the big city to visit us and see the grandchildren. I would always take thirteen- or fourteen-year-old Sheila with me on my round of house calls (yes, those <u>were</u> the days), and what an education she received from the streets that we visited as we made it our joint business to learn more about those sometimes obscure people.

We lived at 12 Beethoven Street, an address that actually thrilled me, besotted as I am with the great master. You would recognize the house—the single story just before you turn down Mozart before you reach Chopin. When we sold our house prior to leaving Vanderbijlpark for pastures new, we moved briefly into 23 Sibelius Street. I could never understand why this address was a source of amusement to several of my acquaintances. Perhaps the gloomy Finnish composer would also have scratched his bald head in puzzlement and then been moved to write a new tone poem evoking vistas of green and a pretty little lake teeming with ducks and geese. He could have called it "Paseo del Lago."

"What's in a name?" asked Juliet. Well, quite a lot if it's the lot you're living in.

THE ART OF DYING

Sudden death is commonplace—the result of war, of accident, of crime and of course of natural causes. Back in 2008, the sudden death by cardiac arrest of the TV personality Tim Russert led to a nationwide outpouring of grief and sorrow from his journalistic peers, the political establishment and the community at large. Not being really aware of his status as a superior television journalist or of his undoubted qualities as an exceptional human being, my thought was that the extreme reaction was perhaps due to the dramatic suddenness of it all.

This led me to consider the various reactions to the prospect of impending death when the event is not sudden. I refer to the responses of both the patient and of those most deeply and closely concerned. My father died when I was four years old, far too young for me to be aware of, let alone to respond to his illness and demise. The first death in the family that I really had to cope with was that of my mother more than forty years later. Having lost her beloved husband to cancer at the early age of fifty-three, my mother always had a dread of that disease, and the very word was not uttered in our house. Euphemisms such as "growth", "lesion", "mass" or "serious condition" were substituted. I should make it clear that in South African society in the middle of the last century, such denial was fairly prevalent and our family's handling of my mother's final illness was by no means unique. Looking back over the fifty years since then, I find almost unbelievable the extent to which we and she engaged in denial. On our part, because of her extreme cancer phobia, we encouraged her to believe that her radiation therapy was to prevent her so-called benign lesion from becoming malignant. On her part, methinks there was a willingness to let us believe that she believed us!

With my wife Ruth's mortal illness in 1984, there was, of course, a much more mature acceptance but as I recall, the truly life and death issues confronting us were still too sensitive and painful for us to have a totally honest last conversation addressing her impending demise and how her courage and state of mind were being affected. Indeed, until very recently I have never managed to really enter into the mind and thoughts of someone dear to me whose fate was sealed. Always, the need to comfort and encourage outweighed facing up to facts. Denial trumped acceptance.

I had a good friend, a medical colleague from more than sixty years ago. Samuel S. and I shared many interests, notably in medicine, music and theater. Our professional paths diverged. Sam became an eminent psychoanalyst after training under Anna Freud in London, while I pursued a career in anesthesiology. Not long before we came to the United States in 1980, Sam and his family emigrated to Adelaide in Australia. Over the ensuing decades we saw each other infrequently on our visits to Australia and on the occasions of our Medical School class reunions here in the US in 1989 and 1999. But we did correspond and spoke occasionally on the phone. In 2006, we heard that Sam was being treated for a malignancy and we managed to speak with his dear wife Jill a few times and just once briefly with Sam himself.

On November 7, 2007, I received an email which in its impact was unique in my personal experience. It read:

...I'm sorry to have to tell you that the duration of my life can now be reduced to weeks rather than months. I can't think of a more appropriate time to say goodbye to you. I don't want to go into the details of my illness. Enough to say that Brian has ensured, if it needed any reinforcement, that the team of oncologists, who are all his partners, have kept me as pain free as possible.

It is a huge handicap to try and communicate over this distance because I'm probably the person who least knows what he wants to say. The words that frequently come to my mind are goodbye and thank you. I have left this letter for several days hoping that my

thoughts would somehow get sorted out. I don't want to hold up the letter any further so I'll send it off now as is.
    Love and best wishes,
    Sam

It was with extreme difficulty that I was able to compose an adequate reply. Excerpts follow:

Sam, this must have been a terribly difficult letter to write, and only a man of great courage could have done so. We are grief stricken at your news and wish so much that we could be closer and able to lend more support. We all go back so far and the memories are so vivid...

We love you and always have. You will never know how important you are to us and the extent to which your warmth, wisdom and compassion have influenced our lives.

We will miss you, dear Sam. We cannot bear to say goodbye, and so we say fare thee well.

I could only marvel then and now at the courage, strength and honesty of a man who had indeed mastered the art of dying.

Samuel S. passed away on December 2, 2007.

Postscript: - This essay was written in 2008. In the ensuing years there have been two developments that have had an influence on my personal responses to the subject of death and dying. The first is that with the passage of time nature takes its toll so that now in 2022 far more of my intimate friends and contemporaries have passed on than are still with us. Inevitably, the impact of yet another loss is blunted and the trauma marginally less painful.

The second and more personal development has been what no parent should have to endure... the loss of a child. Our eldest daughter, in her sixties, was felled by a malignant brain tumor in

August 2019. Grieving though my wife Evette and I still do, I feel that her children and grandchildren have suffered an even greater loss than my own, a loss to which each will have to adjust in their own time in their own way.

The author's late daughter
Chana Cohen
(1952-2019)

WE BOTHERED TO GO TO COMO

As I write this in mid-March 2022, the predominant news worldwide concerns the horrendous events in Ukraine. Amid the torrent of stories of real suffering, I came upon a minor news item that was so crass that it provoked scorn and contempt on my part. A close associate of Vladimir Putin was quoted as bemoaning the fact that European Union sanctions denied him access to both his villas in the northern Italian city of Como.

But this pathetic insensitivity to matters of genuine tragedy did serve to trigger recollections of my only visit to Como in the mid-1960s… lighthearted memories of happier days. Como, a city perched on the southern shore of one of Italy's (and Europe's) most beautiful lakes, is famous for its long history of manufacturing the world's finest silks which earned the soubriquet "Silk City". In addition to the Museo Della Seta dedicated to that history, which was only created decades after our visit, Como boasts a magnificent cathedral and a coastline that is home to the rich and famous (who hasn't heard of George and Amal Clooney?) And then there is the Villa d'Este. This has been one of the world's great hotels, the epitome of luxury, since 1873, although the original structure as the private residence of a cardinal goes all the way back to 1568. The hotel stands on twenty-five acres of lush parkland of breathtaking beauty. The interiors can only be described as palatial. More of that later.

Needless to say, Ruth and I did not stay at Villa d'Este! We were perfectly content with our modest pensione. Our third-floor room boasted a tiny balcony and the hotel had a small pool. I recall with amusement that we planned a swim but the room lacked suitable large towels. The pool attendant understood no English and so I resorted to a charade of a person vigorously drying himself. This prompted what seemed to be an understanding as the attendant nodded, went off, and returned with a can of insecticide spray!

There were signs all over the city announcing a grand fireworks display scheduled for that evening by the lakeshore… "una grande spettacolo pirotecnico". We decided that the view from our balcony would be more than adequate; no need to join the crowd at the shore. Our neighbors in the next room evidently thought otherwise. When the "spettacolo pirotecnico" was well underway we heard what seemed to be a mewling cat in the adjacent room. To our astonishment, we saw a terrified toddler on the balcony next door. While Ruth tried to soothe the child from a distance, I raced down to the office and persuaded the night clerk (fortunately no language problem this time) to open the neighboring door, and Ruth was able to take the screaming child in her arms and comfort him to sleep. And there we remained until, long after the fireworks had ceased, the parents returned. They were a very young couple from the north of England, very grateful, very contrite and obviously very stupid.

There was an amusing sequel to our visit. A week or so later we were on a train in Switzerland and were ear witnesses to the following conversation. We never actually saw the protagonists, but they were clearly two American couples not traveling together but having met, were engaged in a game of one-upmanship. Thus:

> In London, we were at Claridge's
> Oh, we stayed at the Dorchester
> In Paris, we stayed at the Crillon
> Oh, we were at the George V
> In Milan we were at the Grand
> Oh, we stayed at the Excelsior
> In Como, we were at the Villa d'Este
>
> PAUSE
>
> Oh, we didn't bother to go to Como
>
> GAME, SET, MATCH!
>
> Big mistake, Mister! We were glad we did bother.

REQUIEM

"Music is the language of the soul" proudly proclaims the motto of Phoenix's Musical Instruments Museum. William Congreve wrote, "Music hath charms to soothe a savage breast, to soften rocks or bend a knotted oak." The magic of music hath charmed me all the days of my life. Absence of music is inconceivable to me. My tastes have been eclectic—from that total art form known as opera to Gershwin and Porter; from the lieder of Schubert and Schumann to the latter-day lieder of McCartney and Lennon; from practically anything that falls under the rubric of Chamber Music to practically everything by Stephen Sondheim; from the tormented agonies of Shostakovich to the emotional breast beating of Gustav Mahler.

If there is any particular body of work that resonates with me above all others, it is probably the late masterpieces of Beethoven— the late string quartets, piano sonatas and symphonies. But if there is a single work that has impacted me most often and most profoundly, it is none of these. It has to be Giuseppe Verdi's *Requiem*. That a non-believer like Verdi could set the Catholic Requiem Mass so wonderfully and effectively makes it entirely plausible that a non-believer like myself should be so deeply affected by and so involved in its many splendors.

My obsession with the *Requiem* began very early with a recording of the complete work on heaven knows how many 78 r.p.m records. When the new phenomenon called LPs came into being in the 1950s, my very first purchase was Ferenc Fricsay's wonderful performance. The first video version that I saw featured soprano Leontyne Price and a youthful tenor as yet unbearded and quite absurdly slender by the name of Luciano Pavarotti! Early in the present century, my wife Evette and I experienced two profoundly memorable performances of the Verdi *Requiem* within three months of each other, and this is the story of those two moving occasions.

It was the month of June, and we had decided to add a visit to Riga, the capital of Latvia, at the conclusion of an Elderhostel tour of Moscow and St. Petersburg. Evette had a particular interest in seeing Riga for the first time as her family hailed from there and it was the birthplace of two of her older siblings. She had always treasured a visual image of the famed and lovely opera house from her mother's detailed descriptions. So, it suited us very well to make reservations well in advance for a performance of the *Requiem* there on the evening of June 14.

When we arrived in the city, we soon realized that the scheduling of the work for that particular night was not fortuitous. At the impressive and very modern Museum of the Occupation, banners everywhere made clear why June 14 was being commemorated so appropriately. In terms of the infamous agreement between the Soviet Union and Nazi Germany, which had unleashed World War II in 1939, the Baltic States had been absorbed into the USSR. On June 14, 1941, exactly 60 years before our visit, the Russians swooped into Latvia and the other Baltic states, seized and arrested at random thousands of innocent citizens, and deported them in cattle cars to Siberia and almost certain death.

This horrendous event took place just eight days before Nazi Germany invaded the Soviet Union, and it is not really surprising that Latvia's blazing hatred of Russian brutality made a significant number of the public welcome the Germans—at least until it became clear that the fire was even worse than the frying pan! With this poignant history fresh in our minds, the sublime performance of the Requiem in that gem of an opera house made me sure that we would never experience a more emotionally wrenching evening. How wrong I was!

Three months later saw us back in Europe visiting our youngest son David, his wife Drue, and their infant daughter. They had just begun what became a seven-year stay in Brussels. They had planned ahead for our visit and included as a special treat as part of the annual Festival of Flanders a performance of the Verdi *Requiem*

92

in the great Cathedral of Ghent, a forty-five-minute train ride from the capital. More eager anticipation.

Evette and I took the train (one-way tickets) in the morning, planning to tour the ancient city and its various museums and churches, to be joined later by David and Drue for dinner and the concert, after which we would all motor back to Brussels. As he dropped us at the Brussels Central Station, David gave us a cell phone just in case they needed to contact us. The only conceivable reason for a hitch in the plans for the evening was the unlikely event of a babysitter problem. David urged us not to switch on the phone before 5:00 p.m. as the battery was already low. So it was that at 5:00 p.m. David was on the phone with a three-word question: "Have you heard?"

In case you haven't already grasped where I'm going with this tale, the date was Tuesday, the 11th of September, the year was 2001, and 5:00 p.m. in Belgium was 11:00 a.m. in New York City—when the world changed forever. David, involved in the aviation industry, would obviously be in his office for an unpredictable time; our suggestion that we would make our way back to Brussels by train was firmly vetoed, and Drue was already on her way to Ghent to fetch us and bring us safely home. By the time we linked up with her, we had decided to continue with our plans.

Thus it was that three Americans, troubled and bewildered in a strange city in a foreign land, joined the audience for a concert that was not a concert at all but a memorial service for thousands of the dead. Many of our fellow audience members were dressed in black; we all observed a minute's silence before the Requiem began. We all, of course, obeyed the instructions to refrain from any applause at the conclusion and to observe complete silence as we filed out of the historic Cathedral one row at a time.

This time, I must surely be correct in stating that my affinity with Verdi's masterwork could not, cannot, and will not be more firmly cemented.

CRY, MY BELOVED COUNTRIES

The letter arrived just a few days before Christmas, and from the familiar handwriting I assumed it was Bernard's annual Christmas card sent in reply to mine which that year had been mailed rather earlier than usual. But a closer look at the envelope alerted me to the fact that I had assumed incorrectly. The long brown envelope resembled no Christmas card in either shape or color, and the date stamp in Johannesburg showed that it had been sent by surface mail way back in October.

But first let me tell you about Bernard and Catherine Munyai and their mother, Francina. Francina, she of the serene and smiling face, had been our domestic help throughout most of the 1960s—nursemaid to our youngest, cheerful friend to our older children, maid of all work with a propensity for dropping any item that could be dropped, but lovable nonetheless. Francina and her husband, Japie Munyai, had a small house in one of the African townships outside Johannesburg, but she resided in her own neat room attached to our back yard. When she came to work for us, she had a small son, Bernard, who was cared for by his grandmother during Francina's absences at work but who was a frequent and welcome playmate in our home.

When Francina gave up her position to have a second and then a third child she still kept in close touch, and we were delighted when she named her new daughter Catherine in honor of Kathy, our eldest child. Francina died tragically young in 1974, but her widowed husband, Japie, frequently brought the children on weekends to play and to be admired. When in 1977 our Katherine married her own Bernard, the Munyai family were among the invited guests, and there is a cherished photograph of the bridal couple with little Bernard and Catherine, two smart and smiling black kids in their Sunday best.

We lost touch with Japie Munyai and his family when we emigrated to Seattle in early 1980. The next communication was a desperate letter from Bernard at the end of 1984. In sole charge of his siblings since the death of his father three years earlier, he was about to be evicted from the family home that they had occupied as tenants for more than a decade. It appeared that for a relatively trifling sum (but beyond his means) he could purchase the house from the local Township authorities. I still have this letter which arrived the very week that my beloved wife Ruth passed away.

"Please do try to help me," he wrote, "I need your help very much. I know I am demanding too much but I can't help it."

With some difficulty imposed by bureaucratic red tape and geographical distance I was able to secure the purchase of the house and the security that it brought to the young Munyai family. My letter to Bernard after finalizing the affair enclosed a beautiful photograph of my late wife. He had asked how he could thank me, and I set out three things that he could do: He should continue to grow as a good citizen and a credit to his late parents; as the eldest, he should make himself responsible that his younger siblings do the same; and thirdly, he should frame the photograph and treasure it prominently in his home because I regarded what I had done for him as the best possible memorial to the name of Ruth Glauber.

I never saw Bernard again but for the next fifteen years till 1999 we exchanged cards at Christmas. I followed his career with deep satisfaction... graduating high school, enrolling at a Technical College and completing his course there, marrying and cultivating his precious house and garden.

So, I opened this un-festive-looking envelope at this last Christmastime of the twentieth century and found that the familiar looking handwriting was not Bernard's but that of his sister Catherine. She wrote "to inform you that Bernard Munyai was brutally killed in Soweto after he came back from work to find out that his properties were stolen. He confronted those people whom he was suspecting they break into his house. Unfortunately, they beat him to death."

Bernard Munyai was the second young African man in whose personal affairs I had become closely involved. In my grief at Bernard's heartbreaking tragedy, I recalled for the first time in many years my involvement with Simon Gaula. In the early 1950s I was a family practitioner in an industrial town not far from my hometown of Johannesburg. As was the custom in those days of segregation, I had two sets of offices or consulting rooms. One was downtown for white patients and the other was near the black residential township for my African patients. My staff at the latter office consisted of one adult male who acted as interpreter, receptionist and general factotum. No medical or nursing background or skills were required.

One of my favorite patients (and friends) was Richard Gaula, the sole black traffic policeman in the town. He was a handsome and imposing man whose demeanor and smart uniform commanded great respect from all who knew him. Richard's son, Simon, was a bright, tall and gawky teenager in high school. At Richard's request we arranged for Simon to fill in as a substitute for my office assistant during school vacations in order to make extra pocket money. Richard was always carefully attentive that his son's work met expectations. One day in 1956, Simon decided that he had had enough of school and asked to be taken full time into my employ. A family conference of father, son and myself was called. I persuaded them that Simon was far too bright to be buried in the dead-end job that was all I could offer him; that he had the capacity to not only finish high school but to go on to college and possibly become a physician himself one day. If he would stay the course and pass the requirements to enter college, I would undertake to subsidize his Medical School education.

Simon Gaula accepted my offer, devoted himself to his school studies and secured a part-time job at the Post Office on weekends. As a heartbroken Richard Gaula informed me soon thereafter, it was in that capacity that seventeen-year-old Simon was fatally gunned down in an attempted Post Office robbery.

All this came back to me as I tried to grapple with the news of Bernard's senseless murder. What had been so commonplace in the

1950s had become epidemic in the 1990s. What lies ahead for South Africa in the 21st century? With a heavy heart, I can only echo Alan Paton's plaintive call "Cry, the Beloved Country". And what lies ahead for our own beloved country, these violent United States of America?

Postscript: - This essay was written at the turn of the twenty-first century. Now, in 2022, in the wake of the recent massacres in Buffalo, Uvalde, Laguna Woods and Tulsa, and with Columbine, Sandy Hook, Parklands and others burnt into our collective memories, my rhetorical question above becomes ever more pertinent and ever more agonizing.

Made in the USA
Las Vegas, NV
25 August 2022

53955337R00056